Jake's Travel Guides: Istanbul, Turkey

Jake's Travel Guides

Jake Jefferson

Published by Fiel LLC, 2024.

While every precaution has been taken in the preparation of this book, the publisher assumes no responsibility for errors or omissions, or for damages resulting from the use of the information contained herein.

JAKE'S TRAVEL GUIDES: ISTANBUL, TURKEY

First edition. June 3, 2024.

ISBN: 979-8227164414

Written by Jake Jefferson.

Also by Jake Jefferson

Jake's Travel Guides
Jake's Travel Guides: Madrid, Spain
Jake's Travel Guides: Istanbul, Turkey

Table of Contents

Chapter 1: Discovering Istanbul's Rich Heritage

Welcome to Istanbul, Turkey

Istanbul, a city that straddles two continents, awaits you with its blend of rich history and vibrant modernity. As the only city in the world to span both Europe and Asia, separated by the flowing waters of the Bosphorus Strait, Istanbul is a unique and captivating destination.

The history of Istanbul is abundant and diverse, having served as the capital of three great empires: Roman, Byzantine, and Ottoman. This rich past is etched into the city's fabric, evident in its numerous historical landmarks and architectural marvels. The Hagia Sophia stands as a testament to the city's Byzantine glory, transformed from a cathedral to a mosque and now a museum. Nearby, the impressive Blue Mosque dazzles with its six minarets and stunning interior adorned with blue Iznik tiles.

Not far from these iconic structures lies the Topkapi Palace, once the heart of the Ottoman Empire. This sprawling complex offers a glimpse into the opulent lifestyle of sultans, with its lavish rooms, courtyards, and the breathtaking views of the Bosphorus. Delve deeper into Istanbul's past at the Basilica Cistern, an underground wonder once used to store water for the city in times of siege.

Yet, Istanbul is not merely a relic of the past. It thrives as a bustling metropolis where tradition and innovation intersect seamlessly. The Grand Bazaar, one of the largest and oldest covered markets in the world, invites you to explore its maze of shops offering everything from spices and carpets to jewelry and souvenirs. Meanwhile, the modern Istiklal Avenue captivates visitors with its lively atmosphere, dotted with cafes, boutiques, and cultural venues.

Istanbul's culinary scene is as diverse and flavorful as its history. Savor traditional Turkish dishes like kebabs, mezes, and baklava in its myriad of restaurants and street stalls. And do not miss the chance to sample simit, a beloved local snack akin to a sesame-encrusted bagel, typically enjoyed with a cup of strong Turkish tea.

Another dimension of the city is revealed in its Bosphorus cruises. Whether daytime or evening, these cruises offer unparallel views of the skylines and a chance to marvel at iconic sites such as the Dolmabahce Palace, Maiden's Tower, and the Bosphorus Bridge.

Istanbul's cultural vibrancy is reflected in its diverse neighborhoods. Get lost in the winding streets of the historic Sultanahmet district, or soak in the bohemian ambiance of Galata and Karakoy. Each corner of the city tells a story, from the artistic vibes of Cihangir to the upscale allure of Nisantasi.

As a gateway where East meets West, Istanbul is a city of contrasts and complexities, where ancient traditions coexist with modern aspirations. With its dynamic energy, historical wonders, and a kaleidoscope of cultural experiences, Istanbul beckons travelers to lose themselves in its layers and discover its enduring magic.Why Visit Istanbul, Turkey

Istanbul, Turkey, is a city that seamlessly blends the ancient with the modern, offering visitors a unique and captivating travel experience. This metropolis, straddling two continents, Europe and Asia, is a place where history and culture are not just preserved but are very much alive and flourishing. With its rich historical tapestry, vibrant local cuisine, bustling markets, and stunning architectural wonders, Istanbul stands out as a city that must be experienced by any avid traveler.

The city's history is evident at every turn. One of the most iconic landmarks is the Hagia Sophia. Originally built as a cathedral, it later served as a mosque and now stands as a museum, representing Istanbul's rich and diverse history. Nearby, the Blue Mosque with its exquisite blue tiles and six minarets is a testament to the city's Islamic art and architecture. The Topkapi Palace offers a glimpse into the opulent lives of the Ottoman sultans, with its beautifully adorned courtyards, and extensive collections of jewels, and artifacts.

Beyond its historical sites, Istanbul is a treasure trove for food enthusiasts. The local cuisine, a delightful blend of Mediterranean, Middle Eastern, and Central Asian influences, is sure to captivate your taste buds. From the bustling alleys of the Grand Bazaar to the charming restaurants dotting the Bosphorus, you can indulge in an array of dishes, whether it's the succulent kebabs, flavorful mezes, or the sweet, syrupy delights of baklava.

Shopping in Istanbul is an adventure in itself. The Grand Bazaar, one of the oldest and largest covered markets in the world, offers a fascinating array of goods, from handwoven carpets to intricate jewelry and spices. Meanwhile, the Spice Bazaar provides an aromatic journey with its extensive selection of herbs, teas, and sweets.

Istanbul is also a city of contrasts. Modern skyscrapers stand alongside centuries-old palaces, high-end boutiques next to traditional markets. This vibrant clash of old and new is particularly visible in districts like Beyoglu, where contemporary art galleries and cafes coexist with historical buildings. Taking a ferry across the Bosphorus allows you to fully appreciate the city's unique geographical position and the contrasting yet complementary natures of its European and Asian sides.

Moreover, the people of Istanbul are known for their warm hospitality. Whether you are exploring ancient streets, dining in local eateries, or haggling in the markets, you will find the locals to be welcoming and eager to share their culture and history with visitors.

In conclusion, Istanbul is a city that offers something for everyone. Its historical richness, culinary delights, vibrant markets, and the juxtaposition of the traditional with the contemporary make it a compelling destination. Whether you are a history buff, a foodie, a shopaholic, or simply looking to immerse yourself in a culturally rich environment, Istanbul promises an unforgettable experience. Istanbul's allure, captured eloquently in countless pages of literature, serves as the backdrop for our book, a tale that meanders through its historic streets. The city, straddling two continents, Europe and Asia, embodies a melting pot of cultures, history, and modernity. From the towering minarets of the Hagia Sophia to the bustling corridors of the Grand Bazaar, Istanbul is a place where the ancient and the contemporary coexist in a harmonious dance.

The narrative unfolds in neighborhoods such as Sultanahmet, brimming with architectural marvels like the Blue Mosque and Topkapi Palace, each whispering stories of Ottoman grandeur. As we turn the pages, we traverse through Taksim Square, a modern hub of commerce and cosmopolitan life, demonstrating Istanbul's ability to adapt and thrive through centuries of change. The Bosphorus Strait, with its mesmerizing flow, threads the city's heart, symbolizing the interweaving of history and geography in shaping Istanbul's unique identity.

Throughout the book, characters navigate their lives influenced by the city's vibrant spirit. They find themselves at ferry docks and tea houses, in ancient markets and contemporary art galleries, showcasing Istanbul's multifaceted nature. Their journeys, both personal and collective, reflect the complexities of a city that has seen empires rise and fall, yet remains a beacon of resilience and beauty.

As a reader, you are invited to delve into the essence of Istanbul, Turkey, through the eyes of those who call it home. Each chapter weaves the city's rich tapestry, immersing you in a world where every corner has a story to tell and every moment is a testament to the enduring pulse of this magnificent city.

Chapter 2: Discovering Enchanting Istanbul

Istanbul, Turkey, is a city that sits at the crossroads of Europe and Asia, bridging two continents and embodying a rich and diverse history that spans millennia. The city's origins can be traced back to approximately 660 BCE when it was founded by Greek settlers and originally named Byzantium. Over the centuries, Byzantium developed into a significant trading hub, owing to its strategic location along key maritime routes.

In 330 CE, Emperor Constantine the Great declared the city the new capital of the Roman Empire, marking the beginning of its transformation into a cosmopolitan metropolis. Renamed Constantinople, it became a focal point of political power, culture, and commerce. The city's formidable defenses, including the well-known Theodosian Walls, protected it from numerous sieges and invasions.

The fall of the Western Roman Empire left Constantinople as the epicenter of the Byzantine Empire. This era saw the construction of remarkable architectural achievements, such as the Hagia Sophia, which was completed in 537 CE and stood as the world's largest cathedral for nearly a thousand years. Constantinople became a melting pot of diverse cultures, blending Eastern and Western traditions that are still evident in the modern cityscape.

In 1453, Constantinople fell to the Ottoman Turks, a pivotal event that marked the end of the Byzantine Empire and the beginning of a new chapter in the city's history. Renamed Istanbul, it flourished as the capital of the Ottoman Empire. During this period, the city witnessed an influx of various peoples, including Armenians, Greeks, Jews, and others, contributing to its vibrant and multi-ethnic character. The Ottomans also left an indelible mark on the cityscape with monumental structures like the Blue Mosque and Topkapi Palace.

In the early 20th century, following the dissolution of the Ottoman Empire after World War I, Istanbul faced uncertain times. The establishment of the Republic of Turkey in 1923 shifted the capital to Ankara, but Istanbul remained the cultural and economic heartbeat of the nation.

Today, Istanbul is a bustling metropolis that merges its historical legacy with modern advancements. It continues to be a unique blend of the ancient and contemporary, the traditional and the modern, making it a truly global city with a story that continues to unfold with each passing year.Istanbul, Turkey, stands as a city emblematic of significant historical events, serving as a nexus of cultures, religions, and empires. Known as Byzantium and later Constantinople in its storied past, Istanbul bridges Europe and Asia, embodying a unique blend of Eastern and Western influences. The city's strategic location has made it a coveted prize and a pivotal battleground throughout history.

One of the earliest key historical events is the founding of Byzantium in 667 BC by Greek settlers from Megara. This event marked the beginning of the city's long and complex history. Centuries later, the rise of the Roman Empire profoundly impacted the city's development. In 330 AD, Roman Emperor Constantine the Great moved the capital of the Roman Empire to Byzantium, renaming it Constantinople. This transformation marked the beginning of the Byzantine Empire, with Constantinople as its illustrious heart and soul.

Another critical event occurred in 1453 when the Ottoman Empire, led by Sultan Mehmed II, captured Constantinople. This conquest marked the end of the Byzantine Empire, ushering in a new era of Ottoman rule. The city's name gradually transitioned to Istanbul, reflective of its evolving identity. Under Ottoman sovereignty, Istanbul flourished as a center of trade, culture, and politics, leaving an indelible mark on the city's architectural and cultural landscape.

The late 19th and early 20th centuries were a period of upheaval and transformation for Istanbul. The decline of the Ottoman Empire culminated in its dissolution after World War I, leading to the establishment of the Republic of Turkey in 1923. Istanbul, while no longer the capital, remained a significant city in the new nation, symbolizing resilience and continuity through times of change.

In modern times, Istanbul has continued to play a crucial role on the global stage. It has endured and adapted through social, political, and economic shifts, hosting numerous international conferences and serving as a cultural ambassador for Turkey. The city's rich history, marked by key events that shaped its evolution, continues to fascinate historians, travelers, and residents alike.

Ultimately, Istanbul's history is a tapestry woven from centuries of diverse influences and transformative events. Its journey from ancient Byzantium to the flourishing metropolis of Istanbul stands as a testament to its enduring magnetism and pivotal role in world history.Influences on Modern Istanbul, Turkey

Istanbul, the vibrant metropolis that straddles two continents, is a city rich in history and cultural diversity. Over the centuries, it has been shaped by a plethora of influences that have contributed to its unique identity. From its origins as Byzantium to its pivotal role as Constantinople, and finally as Istanbul, the city has continuously evolved while maintaining a blend of the ancient and the contemporary.

One of the key influences on modern Istanbul is its strategic geographical location. Situated at the crossroads of Europe and Asia, Istanbul has long been a melting pot of cultures, ideas, and traditions. This has resulted in a city where East meets West, and where diverse people and traditions coexist. The influence of various empires, notably the Byzantine and Ottoman Empires, is still evident in the city's architecture, cuisine, and everyday life. Landmarks such as the Hagia

Sophia, Topkapi Palace, and the Blue Mosque stand as testaments to the city's rich historical tapestry.

The Ottoman Empire has left a particularly indelible mark on modern Istanbul. As the capital of one of the most powerful empires in history, the city became a center of art, culture, and learning. The architectural style, which features grand domes, minarets, and elaborate tile work, continues to define the cityscape. Moreover, the Ottoman legacy can be experienced in the local cuisine, where dishes such as kebabs, baklava, and Turkish delight are popular staples. The bustling bazaars, such as the Grand Bazaar and the Spice Bazaar, also hark back to the city's illustrious past as a commercial hub.

In addition to its historical influences, Istanbul is also profoundly shaped by its cosmopolitan and modern aspirations. The city has grown into a major global city, attracting millions of tourists and serving as a pivotal economic center. Modern infrastructure projects, such as the Marmaray Tunnel that connects the European and Asian sides of the city, and the new Istanbul Airport, one of the largest in the world, are indicative of the city's rapid development and modernization.

Contemporary Istanbul also boasts a vibrant arts and cultural scene. The city hosts numerous festivals, galleries, and museums that celebrate both its storied past and its dynamic present. The Istanbul Biennial, for instance, is a significant event that draws international artists and art lovers. Additionally, the city's eclectic music and nightlife scene, ranging from traditional Turkish music to contemporary genres, reflects its youthful energy and diverse population.

The influence of secularism and modern Turkish identity, emphasized since the founding of the Republic of Turkey by Mustafa Kemal Ataturk in 1923, has also played a crucial role in shaping modern Istanbul. Ataturk's reforms aimed to modernize and secularize the nation, and their impact is still visible in the city's educational institutions, legal structures, and cultural practices. Istanbul, as

Turkey's largest city, often leads the way in embracing and manifesting these ideals.

In conclusion, modern Istanbul is a city of contrasts and harmonies, where history and contemporary life are intertwined. Influences from its Byzantine and Ottoman past, its strategic geographic location, its role as a leading global city, and the secular reforms of the early 20th century all converge to shape the vibrant and multifaceted character of Istanbul today. As a result, Istanbul remains a fascinating and dynamic city, continually evolving yet deeply rooted in its rich heritage.Local Traditions in Istanbul, Turkey

Istanbul, Turkey, a city that bridges the continents of Europe and Asia, is a vibrant tapestry of cultural richness and diverse traditions. With its unique position as a crossroads of civilizations, the local traditions in Istanbul reflect a blend of historical influences and a deep-rooted heritage.

One of the most cherished traditions in Istanbul is the art of Turkish tea, or çay. Served in slender, tulip-shaped glasses, Turkish tea is more than just a beverage. It is a symbol of hospitality and social interaction. Whether in bustling bazaars, tranquil tea gardens, or cozy homes, the act of drinking tea is accompanied by meaningful conversations and a shared sense of community. Offering tea to guests is a gesture of warmth and friendliness, a tradition that has been passed down through generations.

The culinary traditions of Istanbul are an essential aspect of its cultural fabric. The city is renowned for its diverse and flavorful cuisine, which includes delectable dishes such as kebabs, mezes, and baklava. The aroma of freshly baked simit, a circular bread covered in sesame seeds, wafts through the streets. Likewise, the vibrant street food scene offers an array of delights, from roasted chestnuts to savory köfte. Each meal is a celebration of taste, often accompanied by the ritual of sharing and enjoying food together.

Istanbul is also home to a myriad of traditional arts and crafts. The city's history as a center of trade and craftsmanship is evident in the exquisite carpets, ceramics, and jewelry that are still produced today. The age-old practice of carpet weaving, with its intricate patterns and rich colors, is a testament to the city's artisanal heritage. Similarly, the art of calligraphy adorns many mosques and buildings, showcasing the beauty of the written word.

Religious traditions play a significant role in the daily life of Istanbul's residents. The call to prayer from the city's many mosques, including the iconic Blue Mosque and Hagia Sophia, echoes throughout the city, providing moments of reflection and spirituality. Ramadan, the holy month of fasting, is observed with devotion, culminating in the joyous celebration of Eid al-Fitr, marked by communal prayers, feasts, and festivities.

Festivals and celebrations are deeply ingrained in Istanbul's culture. The city's annual Tulip Festival in April is a vibrant display of thousands of blooming tulips, a flower that holds historical significance in Ottoman culture. During the festival, parks and gardens transform into colorful havens, drawing locals and visitors alike to celebrate the arrival of spring.

Traditional music and dance are also integral to Istanbul's cultural identity. The haunting melodies of classical Turkish music, played on instruments such as the oud and ney, evoke a sense of nostalgia and reverence for the past. Meanwhile, the energetic rhythms of folk dances like the horon and zeybek bring communities together in joyous gatherings.

In essence, the local traditions of Istanbul, Turkey, are a harmonious blend of ancient customs and contemporary practices. They reflect the city's dynamic history, its role as a cultural melting pot, and the enduring spirit of its people. Through these traditions, the essence of Istanbul is preserved and celebrated, creating a tapestry of life that is both colorful and resilient.Istanbul, Turkey is a city that stands at the crossroads of Europe and Asia, embodying a rich mosaic of cultural norms that reflect its diverse history and geographical significance. Understanding the cultural norms of this vibrant metropolis is essential for anyone looking to visit or engage with its inhabitants.

Firstly, respect for traditions and hospitality holds a significant place in the cultural fabric of Istanbul. The city is known for its warm and welcoming nature, where guests are often treated as extended family members. It is common for hosts to offer tea or coffee as a gesture of goodwill, and politely accepting this offer is usually appreciated. Refusing hospitality outright may be seen as discourteous.

Family and social structures in Istanbul tend to be close-knit, with family gatherings and communal activities being integral to daily life. Respect for elders is deeply ingrained, and it is customary to greet older individuals first in social settings. Furthermore, addressing people with appropriate titles such as Bey for men and Hanim for women denotes respect and is often noticed and appreciated.

When it comes to attire, Istanbul presents a blend of modern and traditional values. While the city is progressive and cosmopolitan, modesty in clothing is generally practiced, especially in areas near mosques or during religious occasions. Visitors are advised to dress modestly to respect local customs, especially when visiting religious sites such as the iconic Blue Mosque or Hagia Sophia.

Another vital aspect of Istanbul's cultural norms is the practice of religious observance. Predominantly Muslim, the city's daily rhythm includes the call to prayer heard five times a day. It is important for visitors to be aware of this practice and to show respect by not disturbing those who are observing their religious duties. During the holy month of Ramadan, fasting from dawn to dusk is observed by many, and while visitors are not expected to fast, showing sensitivity to those who are can foster mutual respect.

Language is another essential component of Istanbul's cultural diversity. While Turkish is the official language, many people, particularly in tourist areas, speak English or other languages. Basic phrases in Turkish will go a long way in endearing oneself to the locals and enhancing the overall experience.

Moreover, negotiation and haggling are common practices in Istanbul's bustling bazaars and markets. Shoppers should approach this with a sense of courtesy and good humor, understanding that it is a traditional part of the shopping experience rather than an argument. Developing a knack for friendly bargaining can make shopping more enjoyable and culturally immersive.

In summary, the cultural norms of Istanbul, Turkey are a harmonious blend of tradition and modernity. By understanding and respecting these norms—hospitality, social structures, attire, religious practices, language, and customary interactions—visitors can truly appreciate the richness of Istanbul's cultural landscape while fostering meaningful and respectful exchanges with its residents.Istanbul, Turkey is a city steeped in history and culture. It serves as a bridge between Europe and Asia, blending a myriad of cultural influences that have shaped its identity over millennia. Among its myriad attractions, the city's important cultural institutions stand out as beacons of its rich heritage and vibrant present.

One of the most renowned cultural institutions in Istanbul is the Hagia Sophia. Originally constructed as a cathedral in 537 AD by Emperor Justinian I, it was later converted into a mosque following the Ottoman conquest of Constantinople in 1453. In recent years, it has functioned as a museum and, more recently, has been rededicated as a mosque. The Hagia Sophia's monumental dome and intricate mosaics continue to draw millions of visitors each year, symbolizing the confluence of Christian and Islamic art and architecture.

Another pivotal institution is the Topkapi Palace. This sprawling complex served as the primary residence and administrative center for the Ottoman sultans for nearly 400 years. Within its opulent walls, visitors can explore the imperial halls, kitchens, and treasuries that once housed vast riches and priceless artifacts. The Topkapi Palace is home to the revered Topkapi Dagger and the Spoonmaker's Diamond, two of the world's most famous jewels. The palace also provides a fascinating glimpse into the daily lives and governance of the Ottoman Empire.

The Istanbul Archaeology Museums constitute another cornerstone of the city's cultural landscape. This collection of three separate museums showcases artifacts from the vast expanse of the Ottoman Empire, as well as ancient civilizations that predate Ottoman rule. The Museums house an array of treasures, including the Alexander Sarcophagus and the Treaty of Kadesh, one of the world's earliest known peace agreements. The meticulous curation of these artifacts provides invaluable insights into the ancient world and the shared history of humanity.

For contemporary art enthusiasts, the Istanbul Modern offers an exciting counterpoint to the city's historical institutions. Established in 2004, this museum is dedicated to modern and contemporary Turkish art. Located on the banks of the Bosphorus, it features a dynamic array of exhibitions, from painting and sculpture to photography and multimedia installations. The Istanbul Modern plays a crucial role in promoting Turkish artists on the global stage while fostering a dialogue between Turkish and international art communities.

Another key cultural institution is the Istanbul Foundation for Culture and Arts (IKSV). Founded in 1973, IKSV orchestrates some of the city's most significant cultural events, including the Istanbul Film Festival, Istanbul Music Festival, and Istanbul Biennial. These events draw artists and audiences from around the world, transforming Istanbul into a global hub for artistic innovation and cultural exchange.

Istanbul's important cultural institutions are not merely relics of the past; they are dynamic entities that continue to shape and reflect the city's evolving identity. Through their preservation of history, promotion of the arts, and encouragement of intellectual inquiry, these institutions ensure that Istanbul remains a vibrant center of culture and learning for generations to come.Istanbul, Turkey, a city that straddles two continents, is a vibrant amalgamation of cultures, histories, and modern dynamics. Situated at the crossroads of Europe and Asia, Istanbul serves as a bridge between the East and the West, a role it has played for centuries. The official language of Istanbul, and indeed the entire country, is Turkish. Turkish is a member of the Oghuz branch of the Turkic languages and has a long and intricate history that reflects the diverse influences that have shaped Istanbul over millennia.

Originally, the language developed and spread through the vast territories of the Ottoman Empire. Although the modern Turkish alphabet is derived from the Latin script, it was once written in a version of the Arabic script until the language reform led by Mustafa Kemal Ataturk in the 1920s. This reform was part of a larger set of changes aimed at modernizing Turkey and unifying its various ethnic and linguistic groups under a common identity.

In Istanbul, Turkish is more than just a means of communication; it is a vessel of cultural heritage and identity. It carries the markers of historical epochs from the Byzantine period, when Greek was predominant, through the Ottoman era, when Turkish became the lingua franca, to the present day. Today, Turkish in Istanbul is characterized by a unique blend of traditional and contemporary expressions, enriched by the city's cosmopolitan nature.

While Turkish is the official language, the multicultural tapestry of Istanbul means that other languages like Kurdish, Arabic, Greek, and Armenian are also spoken within various communities. English and other European languages are widely understood, especially in business and tourist areas, reflecting the city's global significance.

Istanbul's language dynamics underscore the city's complex and layered identity. Turkish, in its modern form, serves as a unifying force for residents, fostering a shared sense of belonging in a city that is as diverse as it is ancient. The ability to navigate through a myriad of languages within the city also showcases Istanbul's historic role as a melting pot of civilizations.Traveling to Istanbul, Turkey, can be an incredibly enriching experience. The city is a mosaic of cultures, history, and traditions, and part of that experience is engaging with the local language and customs. While English is widely spoken in many tourist areas, knowing a few common Turkish phrases can significantly enhance your experience and endear you to the locals. These phrases not only help with basic communication but also show respect and appreciation for the culture you are visiting.

One of the most important phrases to know is "Merhaba," which means "Hello". It is a friendly and universal greeting that you can use in any situation. When you meet someone for the first time, saying "Merhaba" sets a positive tone. Likewise, when you are leaving, "Güle güle" means "Goodbye," another warm and respectful phrase to use.

As a traveler, you will frequently find yourself asking for directions or finding specific places. The phrase "Nerede?" means "Where?" and can be coupled with various locations. For instance, if you are looking for the Hagia Sophia, you can ask, "Hagia Sophia nerede?" Similarly, understanding the word "Lütfen," which means "Please," can make your requests more polite. For example, you might say "Bilet lütfen," meaning "Ticket, please," when navigating public transportation.

Understanding numbers and money is crucial in any foreign country. The word for "How much?" is "Ne kadar?". This phrase can help you in markets, restaurants, and shops. If you want to be very polite, you can add "Lütfen" at the end, as in "Ne kadar lütfen?" Additionally, learning the numbers one through ten—bir, iki, üç, dört, beş, altı, yedi, sekiz, dokuz, on—can come in handy for basic transactions.

Eating out is an essential part of the Istanbul experience, famous for its delicious cuisine. When looking at a menu, the word "Menü" is quite universal. After your meal, expressing thanks with "Teşekkür ederim"

(Thank you) can make the interaction more pleasant. If you are in need of assistance, "Yardim eder misiniz?" means "Can you help me?"

For emergencies or critical situations, knowing a few phrases can be beneficial. If you find yourself needing urgent help, "Imdat!" meaning "Help!" can alert those around you. To find a hospital, you could say "Hastane nerede?" which means "Where is the hospital?".

Elevating your travel experience in Istanbul involves more than just visiting landmarks; it includes immersing yourself in the everyday life of the city. Learning and using common phrases will not only aid you in navigation and basic needs but will also create opportunities for meaningful interactions with the locals. By making a small effort to speak Turkish, you open doors to new friendships and deeper insights into this fascinating city. Whether you are exploring the bustling Grand Bazaar or relaxing by the Bosphorus, these common phrases will be invaluable companions on your journey.Istanbul, Turkey is a vibrant city that serves as a cultural and historical bridge between Europe and Asia. For visitors and expatriates navigating the city's linguistic landscape, gaining some familiarity with the local language, Turkish, can significantly enhance the experience. While English is spoken in many tourist areas, a few language tips and resources can help you communicate more effectively and build deeper connections with Istanbul's residents.

First and foremost, learning basic Turkish phrases such as "Merhaba" for hello, "Teşekkür ederim" for thank you, and "Güle güle" for goodbye can go a long way in daily interactions. Polite expressions are highly valued in Turkish culture, and even a basic effort to speak Turkish is often warmly appreciated.

To kickstart your language learning, consider using language apps and online resources. Duolingo, Babbel, and Memrise offer user-friendly platforms that provide foundational vocabulary and grammar. Additionally, YouTube channels like "Learn Turkish with Turkish Class" offer engaging video lessons for all proficiency levels.

For a more immersive experience, language exchange websites such as Tandem or HelloTalk can connect you with native Turkish speakers who might be interested in practicing English in return.

Another excellent resource in Istanbul is the local language schools. Institutions like the Istanbul Language Center and the International House Istanbul offer structured courses ranging from beginner to advanced levels. These classes not only focus on language proficiency but also provide insights into Turkish culture and customs, which can be invaluable for newcomers.

Participating in local conversation clubs or meetups can also be a great way to practice speaking Turkish in a casual, social setting. Websites like Meetup and Couchsurfing often list events where language enthusiasts gather to practice multiple languages, including Turkish. This can be a fun and interactive way to improve your language skills while making new friends.

Lastly, do not underestimate the value of everyday practice. Engaging in conversations with shopkeepers, asking for directions, or ordering food in Turkish can be excellent opportunities to apply what you have learned. Istanbul's lively bazaars, bustling cafes, and scenic parks provide countless chances to immerse yourself in the language.

In conclusion, while Istanbul is accommodating to English speakers, learning Turkish can significantly enrich your experience in the city. Utilizing language apps, enrolling in local language courses, joining conversation clubs, and practicing daily interactions can help you navigate Istanbul with greater ease and cultural understanding. Embracing the local language not only fosters better communication but also opens doors to a deeper, more authentic engagement with Istanbul's rich heritage and warm-hearted people.

Chapter 3: Istanbul Trip Planning Essentials

Istanbul, Turkey is a city of remarkable charm and intricate history, drawing visitors from all corners of the globe. One of the key aspects to understand when planning a trip to Istanbul is its peak seasons, which can greatly affect the traveler experience.

Peak tourist seasons in Istanbul typically span from late spring through the early fall, encapsulating the months of May, June, July, August, and September. During these times, the city embraces a warm and inviting climate, with temperatures often ranging between 20 to 30 degrees Celsius. The appealing weather conditions make it ideal for exploring Istanbul's plethora of outdoor attractions, such as the bustling Grand Bazaar, the majestic Hagia Sophia, and the serene Bosphorus Strait. The city during these months is vibrant and full of life, with street festivals, open-air concerts, and lively markets adding to Istanbul's dynamic atmosphere.

Another popular peak period is around major festivals and holidays. Ramadan, for instance, brings a unique cultural significance to Istanbul. Although the exact dates vary each year, this period of fasting and feasting culminates in the festive celebrations of Eid, where the city comes alive with nightly events, special prayers, and communal meals. Similarly, Turkish Republic Day on October 29 and International Workers' Day on May 1 are marked by parades, fireworks, and public festivities.

However, the influx of tourists during peak seasons also means that popular sites can become crowded, and accommodation prices tend to surge. Advanced booking is often necessary to secure the best rates and experiences. Exploring lesser-known areas and hidden gems can also provide respite from the busiest spots while still offering a deep dive into the rich tapestry of Istanbul's culture and history.

Shoulder seasons, such as early spring in April or late fall in October, offer an attractive alternative for those looking to avoid the peak crowds while still enjoying mild weather and ripe opportunities for sightseeing. These times frame the city in softer light and cooler temperatures, allowing for a more leisurely and contemplative exploration of Istanbul's historic treasures and modern vibes.

Winter, while not typically categorized as a peak season, also holds its own unique appeal. From November through March, the city is quieter, and the chillier weather brings a different kind of beauty to Istanbul. Snow-blanketed rooftops and the mist over the Bosphorus provide a peaceful backdrop for a cozy and intimate experience. During this time, visitors can enjoy the city's indoor attractions and warm up with traditional Turkish tea and sumptuous meals at local taverns.

In conclusion, understanding the peak seasons in Istanbul is essential for curating a personal and rewarding travel experience. Whether drawn by the vibrant summer activities, the solemn beauty of cultural festivities, or the quiet charm of off-season months, each period offers a unique perspective of this mesmerizing city. Off-Season Benefits: Istanbul, Turkey

Traveling to Istanbul, Turkey during the off-season offers numerous benefits that can redefine one's entire experience of this remarkable city. While summer is typically the peak season for tourism, visiting during the less crowded months can provide a truly unique and enriching adventure.

One of the most significant advantages of visiting Istanbul in the off-season is the reduced number of tourists. Major attractions like the Hagia Sophia, the Blue Mosque, and the Topkapi Palace are much less crowded, allowing visitors to enjoy these historical landmarks without the overwhelming throngs of people. This means more time to linger, appreciate, and take in the beauty and history that these sites offer.

Moreover, the off-season usually brings about milder weather, particularly in the autumn and spring months. The sweltering heat of the summer gives way to pleasant temperatures, making it a joy to explore the city on foot. This is the perfect time to wander through the cobblestone streets of Sultanahmet, discover hidden gems in the bazaars, or take a leisurely cruise on the Bosphorus without the discomfort of extreme heat.

Another benefit of traveling to Istanbul in the off-season is the potential for lower accommodation costs. Hotels and Airbnb properties often lower their rates during these periods to attract more visitors. This can make staying in some of the city's more luxurious accommodations more affordable, enhancing the overall comfort and experience. Along with cheaper lodging, tourists may also find fewer queues and wait times at popular restaurants and eateries, enabling them to indulge in Istanbul's famous cuisine with greater ease.

Shopping in Istanbul during the off-season is another delightful experience. The Grand Bazaar and the Spice Bazaar, which are usually packed during peak months, are relatively calm. This allows for a more relaxed shopping experience where one can engage more personally with the vendors, negotiate better prices, and take more time to appreciate the craftsmanship of the goods offered.

Finally, the off-season provides an excellent opportunity to engage more deeply with the local culture. With fewer tourists around, it becomes easier to connect with locals, understand their way of life, and participate in daily activities. Whether you are sipping Turkish tea at a local café, enjoying a traditional meal, or exploring neighborhood markets, the off-season offers a more authentic and enriching cultural experience.

In summary, visiting Istanbul during the off-season presents a wealth of benefits. From reduced crowds and milder weather to lower costs and deeper cultural engagements, the quieter months can make for a more relaxed and intimate exploration of one of the world's most fascinating cities.Weather Overview

Istanbul, Turkey is a city of remarkable diversity and historical significance, located at the crossroads of Europe and Asia. The city's weather is equally varied, offering a range of climates throughout the year that reflect its unique geographic position. Istanbul experiences four distinct seasons, each bringing its own unique character to the city.

Spring, spanning from March to May, is one of the most pleasant times to visit Istanbul. During this season, the city blossoms with colorful flowers and lush greenery. Temperatures are mild, typically ranging from 10 to 20 degrees Celsius. Rainfall is moderate, and the occasional showers help maintain the verdant landscape. Spring in Istanbul is often heralded by blooming tulips, which are celebrated in festivals and parks around the city.

Summer, lasting from June to August, brings warmer weather and longer days. Temperatures can rise significantly, often reaching up to 30 degrees Celsius, with occasional peaks even higher. Despite the heat, the city's proximity to the Bosphorus Strait provides a refreshing breeze, especially in the evenings. Summers in Istanbul are characterized by dry conditions, making it a popular time for both locals and tourists to enjoy the city's many outdoor attractions, including its beautiful beaches and historical sites.

Autumn, from September to November, transforms Istanbul into a canvas of rich, warm colors. The weather remains relatively mild with temperatures ranging from 15 to 25 degrees Celsius. Rain begins to increase during this season, preparing the city for the winter ahead. The pleasant weather and reduced crowds make autumn an ideal time for exploring Istanbul's cultural treasures and scenic views.

Winter in Istanbul, which spans from December to February, is often cool and damp. Temperatures usually fluctuate between 3 to 10 degrees Celsius, but can occasionally dip below freezing. Snow is not uncommon, transforming the city's iconic landmarks into a winter wonderland. Rainfall is more frequent in this season, making the city streets glisten. Although winter might be less appealing to some, it offers a unique and quieter experience of Istanbul's beauty.

Overall, Istanbul's weather is as dynamic and captivating as the city itself. The changing seasons ensure that there is always something new and intriguing to experience, no matter when one decides to visit. Whether basking in the summer sun or enjoying the quiet charm of a snowfall, Istanbul's diverse climate enhances its allure as a city that seamlessly blends the ancient with the modern.Entry Requirements for Istanbul, Turkey

Traveling to Istanbul, Turkey, a city straddling Europe and Asia, is an exciting adventure that combines rich history, vibrant culture, and stunning architecture. However, before packing your bags and heading off to this captivating metropolis, it is essential to understand the entry requirements to ensure a smooth journey.

Firstly, travelers must be aware of the visa requirements. Citizens of many countries need to obtain a visa before entering Turkey. The process has been simplified with the introduction of the e-Visa system, which allows eligible nationals to apply online. The application is straightforward, usually requiring a valid passport, a credit card for payment, and an email address. Once approved, the e-Visa is sent via email and must be printed out or saved on a mobile device for presentation upon arrival.

It is important to note that the requirements may vary based on nationality. Citizens of some countries are permitted to enter Turkey visa-free for short stays, typically up to 90 days within a 180-day period, while others may have different regulations. Therefore, it is advisable to check the latest information from the Turkish Ministry of Foreign Affairs or contact the nearest Turkish consulate or embassy well in advance of travel.

In addition to visa requirements, travelers should ensure their passports are valid for at least six months beyond their intended departure date from Turkey. Immigration officials are strict about this regulation, and it is a fundamental part of the entry process.

Health and safety have also become focal points in recent times. Due to global health concerns, there may be additional requirements such as proof of vaccination, negative COVID-19 test results, or health declaration forms. These measures aim to safeguard both visitors and residents. Travelers should keep themselves updated on current health advisories and protocols by consulting official health department websites or their airline.

Moreover, it is crucial to have proof of onward travel, such as a return ticket or an itinerary detailing travel plans following the stay in Istanbul. While not always requested, having this documentation can smooth the entry process if questioned by immigration authorities.

Lastly, possessing sufficient funds for the duration of the stay can also be a requirement. Visitors might be asked to demonstrate financial stability to ensure they can support themselves during their visit. This can be in the form of bank statements, credit cards, or traveler's cheques.

In summary, when planning a trip to Istanbul, Turkey, understanding the entry requirements is vital. This includes obtaining the appropriate visa, ensuring passport validity, staying informed about health protocols, and having documentation for onward travel and financial support. With proper preparation, travelers can look forward to an incredible experience in one of the world's most historic and culturally rich cities.Istanbul, Turkey, is a city of rich history and vibrant culture, attracting millions of visitors each year. To ensure a smooth and hassle-free experience when visiting this magnificent city, it is essential to be well-prepared and have all the necessary documents in order.

First and foremost, a valid passport is a must for entering Istanbul, Turkey. Visitors should ensure that their passport is up-to-date and will remain valid for at least six months beyond their intended stay. It is advisable to have a few photocopies of the passport on hand in case the original is lost or stolen.

In addition to a passport, most travelers will need a visa to enter Turkey. The process for obtaining a visa can vary depending on one's nationality. Citizens of certain countries can apply for an e-Visa online, which is a quick and convenient option. The e-Visa application typically requires basic personal information, passport details, and the payment of a fee. Once approved, the e-Visa will be sent via email and should be printed out and carried during the trip. Nationals of some countries may be eligible for a visa-free entry or visa-on-arrival, but it is important to check the most current regulations before traveling.

Travelers should also have a confirmed return or onward ticket as proof of their intention to leave the country within the allowed period of stay. Additionally, it is prudent to carry proof of accommodation arrangements, such as hotel reservations or a letter of invitation from a host in Istanbul.

Health insurance is another important document to consider. While it is not a mandatory requirement for entry, having comprehensive travel health insurance can save travelers from significant medical expenses in case of illness or accident. It is wise to carry a copy of the insurance policy and contact details for easy reference.

For those planning on driving in Istanbul, an international driving permit (IDP) in addition to a valid home country driving license may be required. It is essential to familiarize oneself with Turkish traffic rules and regulations to ensure safe driving practices while navigating the city's bustling streets.

Lastly, it is advisable to have some local currency on hand for immediate expenses upon arrival. While credit cards are widely accepted, having Turkish lira for small purchases, transportation, and tips can be convenient. Currency exchange services are available at the airport, banks, and currency exchange offices throughout the city.

In conclusion, being well-prepared with the necessary documents can greatly enhance the experience of visiting Istanbul, Turkey. Ensuring that one has a valid passport, the appropriate visa, proof of onward travel, accommodation details, health insurance, and an international driving permit if needed, will help ensure a smooth and enjoyable trip to this captivating city.Health and Safety Advisories in Istanbul, Turkey

Visiting Istanbul, Turkey, offers travelers a unique blend of history, culture, and modernity. Nestled between Europe and Asia, Istanbul is a city with rich traditions and a vibrant atmosphere. While it promises an unforgettable experience, it is vital for visitors to stay informed about health and safety advisories to ensure a smooth and enjoyable trip.

Health advisories for Istanbul emphasize the importance of vaccinations. Before traveling to Istanbul, it is recommended to be up-to-date with routine vaccines such as measles, mumps, rubella, diphtheria, tetanus, and polio. Additionally, the Hepatitis A and B vaccines are suggested due to potential exposure through food or water. Travelers may also consider the typhoid vaccine, especially if planning to venture into more rural areas or eat street food. It is always wise to consult a healthcare provider several weeks before departure to address any other specific health concerns or required medications.

Water and food safety are critical aspects to consider. Tap water in Istanbul is generally not advised for drinking. Bottled water is widely available and should be used for both drinking and brushing teeth. When it comes to food, Istanbul is renowned for its cuisine, which ranges from upscale restaurants to street vendors selling delicious local fare. Eating at busy establishments with high turnover is usually a good indicator of food quality. Be cautious with raw or undercooked foods to avoid any potential health risks.

Safety advisories highlight that Istanbul is a large city with the same precautions one would take in any major metropolis. Petty crime, such as pickpocketing and bag snatching, can occur, especially in crowded areas like markets, public transportation, and tourist sites. It is prudent to carry only necessary items, keep valuables in a secure and hidden place, and remain vigilant.

When navigating Istanbul, use registered taxis or recognized ride-sharing apps for transportation. Public transportation, including the metro, trams, and buses, is extensive and generally safe but can be crowded during peak times. Always be aware of your surroundings, and avoid showing signs of affluence which might attract unwanted attention.

Political demonstrations and protests can occur in Istanbul. While most are peaceful, it is advisable to avoid large gatherings and stay informed about current events through reliable news sources and local advisories. In the unlikely event of an emergency, visitors should be aware of where their country's embassy or consulate is located.

Healthcare facilities in Istanbul are advanced and accessible, particularly in the central parts of the city. It is important to have travel insurance that covers medical expenses and emergency evacuations. In case of minor health issues, there are numerous pharmacies available that provide both over-the-counter and prescribed medications.

In summary, Istanbul invites travelers to explore its remarkable blend of cultures, history, and architectural marvels. By keeping informed about health and safety advisories—covering vaccinations, food and water hygiene, petty crime, political awareness, and healthcare facilities—visitors can enjoy a safe and healthy visit to this enchanting city.Flights to Istanbul, Turkey

Istanbul, Turkey, is a city that seamlessly interweaves the fabric of ancient traditions with the vivacity of modern life. Spanning two continents, Europe and Asia, Istanbul is a unique city that offers a rich tapestry of cultures, cuisines, and histories. Booking a flight to Istanbul means embarking on a journey to one of the world's most captivating destinations.

As the plane descends, passengers are often struck by the breathtaking view of Istanbul's coastline and its iconic landmarks such as the Hagia Sophia, the Blue Mosque, and the Bosphorus Strait. Once you land, the city's vibrant energy becomes immediately apparent. The bustling streets, filled with the sounds of calls to prayer from centuries-old minarets, blend harmoniously with the modern beat of urban life.

For history enthusiasts, Istanbul is a treasure trove. The city's storied past stretches over millennia, from its days as Byzantium and Constantinople to its current incarnation. Visitors can explore ancient palaces, mosques, and bazaars. The Topkapi Palace, once home to Ottoman sultans, and the awe-inspiring Basilica Cistern are just two examples of the many historical sites awaiting discovery.

Culinary adventurers will find themselves equally delighted by Istanbul. The city's cuisine is as diverse as its history, offering an array of flavors from traditional kebabs and mezes to contemporary fusion dishes. Street food is a particularly delightful experience; a taste of simit, a type of sesame-covered bread, or a sip of Turkish tea provides an authentic taste of daily life in Istanbul.

Istanbul's charm goes beyond its historical and culinary offerings. The city's natural beauty is also a significant draw. Visitors can take a scenic cruise along the Bosphorus Strait, which provides stunning views of both the European and Asian sides of the city. The Princes' Islands, a short ferry ride away, offer a peaceful retreat from the city's hustle and bustle.

Flights to Istanbul are readily available from numerous international locations, reflecting the city's status as a major travel hub. Istanbul's unique blend of East and West, old and new, makes it an alluring destination for travelers of all types. Whether you are drawn by its rich history, diverse food, or scenic vistas, a flight to Istanbul promises an unforgettable experience.

In conclusion, Istanbul is a city that defies simple description. It is a place where the past and present coexist in perfect harmony, offering endless discoveries to those willing to explore. Booking a flight to Istanbul is more than just travel; it is an invitation to experience a world where every moment is infused with the magic of history and the vitality of today.Istanbul, Turkey, renowned for its rich history and cultural heritage, boasts an extensive and efficient network of train and bus services that facilitate seamless urban mobility for both residents and visitors. The city's transportation system is designed to cater to the needs of its dynamic and ever-growing population while allowing tourists to explore its myriad attractions with ease.

The backbone of Istanbul's public transportation is its comprehensive train system. The metro network, known as the Istanbul Metro, features several lines that crisscross the city, connecting key districts and neighborhoods. The metro is complemented by the Marmaray, a remarkable rail project that links the European and Asian sides of the city via a tunnel beneath the Bosphorus Strait. This feat of engineering significantly reduces travel times and enhances connectivity between the two continents. Each train is modern, clean, and equipped with amenities designed to ensure a comfortable journey.

Beyond the metro and Marmaray, Istanbul's suburban train service, the TCDD Taşıma, provides additional reach to more remote areas. These trains are an indispensable mode of transport for daily commuters and those who travel longer distances within the metropolitan area. Moreover, the historical tramlines, including the nostalgic trams of Taksim and Kadıköy, offer not just transit services but also a picturesque glimpse into the city's past.

Complementing the rail services is a robust network of buses managed by the Istanbul Electric Tram and Tunnel Company, or IETT. The bus system covers vast stretches of the city, reaching areas that are not serviced by the metro or trams. Buses operate from early in the morning until late at night, ensuring that all areas of Istanbul remain accessible at virtually any time of day. The fleet includes a variety of bus types, from standard-sized buses to large capacity vehicles for busy routes, all designed to provide a reliable and convenient travel experience.

The city's commitment to public transportation is further evident in its adherence to schedules and frequent updates to services to meet the growing demands of the population. Istanbulkart, a rechargeable transit card, simplifies the fare system across all modes of transportation, enabling seamless transfers between buses, trains, and ferries.

In summary, Istanbul's train and bus services are integral to the city's infrastructure, ensuring that its bustling populace and the throngs of tourists can navigate its stunning landscape with minimal hassle. This intricate network of trains and buses not only highlights Istanbul's modernity but also respects its storied past, reflecting a city that harmoniously blends the old with the new.Local Transportation Overview: Istanbul, Turkey

Istanbul, Turkey is a city of immense historical significance and vibrant modern life, bridging two continents—Europe and Asia. It boasts a diverse and efficient local transportation network that caters to its sprawling population and teeming visitors. Navigating this bustling metropolis can be an adventure in itself, given the variety of transportation options available.

The backbone of Istanbul's transportation system is the extensive bus network, managed by the Istanbul Electricity, Tramway and Tunnel General Management (IETT). With hundreds of routes crisscrossing the city, buses offer an affordable means of travel to nearly every corner of Istanbul. For those looking to avoid the infamous traffic congestion, Istanbul also offers a robust metro system. The city's Metro Istanbul network continues to expand, providing a fast and reliable way to commute across key districts. Currently, the metro network includes multiple lines covering both the European and Asian sides of the city, with regular expansions underway.

In addition to the metro and bus services, the historical tramway is a charming and efficient way to explore parts of Istanbul. The most famous of these is the T1 Kabatas-Bagcilar tramline, which runs through many of the city's major historical and commercial districts. Another unique feature of Istanbul's public transport is the nostalgic tram on Istiklal Street, offering a picturesque journey reminiscent of the city's past.

For travel across the Bosphorus, Istanbul has an impressive array of ferry services. These ferries connect the European side to the Asian side and provide a scenic and leisurely route for crossing the strait. Complementing the ferry system is the Marmaray, a contemporary rail tunnel under the Bosphorus, that links both sides of the city seamlessly.

Moreover, Istanbul has an advanced metrobüs system, a dedicated bus rapid transit route that withstands the traffic delays common in the city. The metrobüs operates on a special reserved lane and can significantly cut down travel time, especially during rush hours.

For those who prefer private transport, taxis are readily available throughout the city. However, it is advisable to choose registered taxis to avoid any potential issues with fare discrepancies. Given the increasing adoption of technology, ride-sharing apps such as BiTaksi and Uber have also gained popularity, providing another convenient option to navigate the city.

Cycling is slowly gaining traction in Istanbul, although the hilly nature and sometimes congested streets can pose challenges. The city has been gradually enhancing cycling infrastructure in an effort to encourage this eco-friendly mode of transport.

Ultimately, Istanbul's variety of transportation modes makes it possible for residents and tourists alike to navigate the city's many wonders with relative ease. The blend of traditional methods and modern systems reflects Istanbul's unique cultural tapestry and its ongoing march towards urban modernization. Whether traveling by land, sea, or underground, moving through Istanbul is as diverse and dynamic as the city itself.

Chapter 4: Staying in Istanbul's Splendor

Istanbul, Turkey, is a city that effortlessly bridges the gap between Europe and Asia, both geographically and culturally. It is a vibrant metropolis where the rich tapestry of history meets the dynamic energy of modern life. For visitors, this captivating city offers an array of experiences, and one of the most crucial aspects of any travel plan is finding the perfect place to stay. Fortunately, Istanbul is home to a multitude of hotels that cater to a wide range of preferences and budgets, each promising a unique slice of the city's charm and hospitality.

For those seeking opulence and luxury, the city boasts several five-star hotels that offer top-tier amenities and world-class service. These establishments, often located in the heart of historic districts or along the picturesque Bosphorus Strait, provide not only a lavish stay but also breathtaking views of the city's iconic landmarks. From the grandeur of the Hagia Sophia and the Blue Mosque to the bustling Grand Bazaar and the serene beauty of the Bosphorus, guests at these hotels have the city's treasures right at their doorstep.

Boutique hotels in Istanbul present a different but equally enchanting experience. These smaller establishments are often housed in restored Ottoman-era buildings, exuding a unique charm and intimacy. Staying in a boutique hotel allows visitors to immerse themselves in the local culture and history, as these hotels often reflect the rich architectural and artistic heritage of Istanbul. Each room is typically decorated with traditional Turkish elements, and the personalized service ensures a memorable and authentic stay.

For travelers on a budget, Istanbul also offers a variety of affordable hotels and hostels without compromising on comfort or location. Many of these budget-friendly options are conveniently situated in central areas like Sultanahmet, Beyoglu, and Kadikoy, providing easy access to major attractions and public transportation. Despite their lower cost, these accommodations often come with modern amenities, including free Wi-Fi, complimentary breakfast, and comfortable, clean rooms that provide a restful sanctuary after a day of exploring the city.

Families visiting Istanbul will find a selection of family-friendly hotels that offer spacious rooms and suites, child-friendly facilities, and a welcoming atmosphere. Many of these hotels provide additional services such as babysitting, kids' clubs, and recreational activities, ensuring that both parents and children have a pleasant and stress-free stay. The convenient locations of these hotels allow families to easily visit kid-friendly attractions like the Istanbul Aquarium, Miniaturk, and the Rahmi M. Koc Museum.

In conclusion, Istanbul's diverse range of hotels reflects the city's multifaceted character and the varied needs of its visitors. Whether seeking luxury, boutique charm, budget-friendly options, or family accommodations, travelers will find a hotel that perfectly aligns with their preferences. Each stay promises to be an integral part of the unforgettable experience that is Istanbul, a city where history, culture, and modernity converge in a spectacular fashion.Istanbul, Turkey is one of the world's most captivating and historically rich cities. It serves as a bridge between Europe and Asia, combining a tapestry of cultures and traditions that have been shaped over centuries. In this vibrant city, travelers from all walks of life can find welcoming and affordable accommodation in the numerous hostels that dot its bustling neighborhoods.

Hostels in Istanbul offer a unique way to experience the city. They provide not only budget-friendly lodging options but also a sense of community and camaraderie among guests. Many of these hostels are situated in prime locations, allowing easy access to the city's famous landmarks and attractions. For example, Sultanahmet hosts an array of hostels with close proximity to iconic sites like the Hagia Sophia, Blue Mosque, and Topkapi Palace. Staying in this area allows visitors to explore the historical heart of Istanbul on foot, making it an ideal choice for history enthusiasts.

In addition to their convenient locations, hostels in Istanbul often feature a range of amenities designed to make stays comfortable and enjoyable. Common communal areas such as lounges, kitchens, and rooftop terraces provide perfect settings for socializing and meeting fellow travelers. Many hostels also organize events like guided city tours, cultural nights, and pub crawls, offering guests opportunities to delve deeper into Istanbul's diverse culture and vibrant nightlife.

The city is also known for its warm hospitality, and this extends to the hostels. Local staff often go above and beyond to provide valuable tips and recommendations, ensuring that guests can make the most out of their visit. From suggesting hidden gems in the city to helping with transportation, the personal touch provided by hostel staff can significantly enhance the travel experience.

Istanbul's hostels attract a wide variety of travelers, including solo adventurers, groups of friends, and even families. The diversity of guests creates a dynamic and inclusive atmosphere where people from different cultures and backgrounds can connect and share their travel experiences. This aspect of hostel culture fosters a spirit of global community that is particularly strong in a cosmopolitan city like Istanbul.

Moreover, hostels cater to different preferences and needs. Whether it is a cozy dormitory for someone seeking an economical option or a private room for those wanting extra privacy, there are accommodations to suit every type of traveler. Some hostels even capture the city's historic essence with charming architecture and traditional decor, allowing guests to immerse themselves in Istanbul's unique ambiance immediately upon arrival.

In conclusion, hostels in Istanbul, Turkey offer much more than just a place to sleep. They provide an enriching experience that combines affordability, socialization, and accessibility to the city's many wonders. As the gateway to exploring both Eastern and Western cultures, staying in an Istanbul hostel ensures that travelers can fully experience the magic of this extraordinary city.Vacation Rentals in Istanbul, Turkey

Istanbul, Turkey is a city that seamlessly bridges the gap between continents and cultures, blending the best of both East and West. As one of the most historically and culturally rich cities in the world, Istanbul has become an increasingly popular destination for travelers seeking an immersive experience. One of the best ways to experience the city's charm is through vacation rentals, which offer a unique and personal way to enjoy all that Istanbul has to offer.

Vacation rentals in Istanbul come in various forms, catering to different tastes and budgets. From luxurious apartments with breathtaking views of the Bosphorus to cozy flats nestled in the historic neighborhoods of Sultanahmet and Beyoglu, there is something for everyone. These rental properties provide a home-like atmosphere, allowing visitors to live like locals and experience the city in a more intimate manner than traditional hotels might offer.

Staying in a vacation rental allows travelers to explore Istanbul at their own pace. Many rentals are conveniently located near major attractions, such as the Blue Mosque, Hagia Sophia, and Topkapi Palace, making it easy to walk to these iconic sites. Additionally, vacation rentals often come equipped with kitchens, providing the opportunity to shop at local markets and prepare meals with fresh, local ingredients. This not only saves money but also adds another layer to the cultural experience by allowing visitors to experiment with Turkish cuisine.

Moreover, vacation rentals can provide a sense of privacy and comfort that is often lacking in crowded hotels. Whether it is a modern apartment in the bustling district of Taksim or a charming townhouse in the quieter area of Kadikoy on the Asian side, guests can enjoy personal space and amenities tailored to their needs. Many rentals also include features such as Wi-Fi, laundry facilities, and even private balconies or terraces, enhancing the overall experience.

For those traveling in groups or with family, vacation rentals can be particularly advantageous. Larger apartments or houses can accommodate multiple people under one roof, offering communal spaces for socializing and bonding. This is not only more economical but also creates a more cohesive and enjoyable travel experience.

In conclusion, vacation rentals in Istanbul, Turkey offer an excellent way to fully experience the vibrancy and history of this remarkable city. With options to suit all preferences and needs, these rentals provide comfort, privacy, and the chance to live like a local. Whether staying for a few days or a few weeks, vacation rentals are an appealing choice for anyone looking to immerse themselves in the unique charm of Istanbul.Istanbul, Turkey is a vibrant metropolis that marries the ancient with the contemporary, creating a unique environment that entices travelers from around the world. Among the myriad attractions that the city offers, its boutique options stand out for providing an intimate and personalized experience, immersing visitors into the local culture while maintaining a level of luxury and comfort.

Walking through the historic districts of Istanbul, one can find a plethora of boutique hotels, each with its own distinct charm. Many of these establishments are nestled in refurbished Ottoman-era mansions, offering an authentic glimpse into the architectural splendor of the past. These boutique hotels often boast regal interiors adorned with traditional Turkish decor, from handwoven carpets to intricate tile work, transporting guests to a bygone era while ensuring modern amenities are at their disposal.

In neighborhoods like Sultanahmet and Beyoglu, the boutique experience is notably enriched by the proximity to iconic landmarks. One can stay mere steps away from the awe-inspiring Hagia Sophia or the majestic Topkapi Palace. The convenience of these locations allows for leisurely exploration of the nearby bazaars, cafes, and historic sites, ensuring that the essence of Istanbul is never more than a short stroll away.

Beyond accommodations, Istanbul's boutique options extend to dining and shopping as well. The city is home to an array of chic eateries that blend traditional Turkish flavors with contemporary cooking techniques. These restaurants often prioritize the use of locally sourced ingredients, creating dishes that are both fresh and faithful to the rich culinary heritage of the region. For those looking to take home a piece of Istanbul, the city's boutique shops offer everything from handcrafted jewelry to bespoke fashion items, letting travelers acquire unique souvenirs that reflect the artisanal talents of local craftsmen.

The allure of Istanbul's boutique options lies not just in their physical offerings, but in the personalized service they provide. Boutique establishments, by virtue of their smaller size and localized management, are able to offer an unparalleled level of attention to detail. Guests are often treated to customized itineraries, private tours, and insider tips that cater to their individual interests, making each stay a bespoke experience.

In conclusion, the boutique options in Istanbul, Turkey provide a harmonious blend of luxury, culture, and personalized service. Whether through charming hotels, exquisite dining, or unique shopping experiences, these options allow visitors to experience the city in a way that is both authentic and indulgent. Istanbul's boutique scene encapsulates the city's spirit, offering an intimate glimpse into its rich history and vibrant present. Istanbul, Turkey is a city of incredible diversity and historical richness, straddling two continents and presenting a unique juxtaposition of the old and new. Each of its neighborhoods offers a distinct character and cultural experience, painting a vivid mosaic of life in this vibrant metropolis.

The historic heart of Istanbul lies in Sultanahmet, a neighborhood renowned for its iconic landmarks. Here, the grandeur of the Hagia

Sophia and the intricate beauty of the Blue Mosque stand as testaments to the city's Byzantine and Ottoman legacies. This area is heavily frequented by tourists, who flock to explore the Topkapi Palace and roam the ancient streets that whisper tales of empires gone by.

Moving across the Golden Horn, one encounters the bustling neighborhood of Beyoglu, famous for its lively Istiklal Avenue. This pedestrian thoroughfare pulses with energy day and night, lined with shops, cafes, and historical buildings. Taksim Square, at the heart of Beyoglu, serves as a central hub for cultural and political events. The district's artistic soul reveals itself in places like the Pera Museum, while the Galata Tower offers panoramic views of the cityscape, capturing the essence of a place where tradition meets modernity.

Karakoy and Galata, historically significant ports, have rapidly transformed into trendy districts attracting a hip crowd. Art galleries, boutique hotels, and chic eateries have given these neighborhoods a contemporary flair while maintaining an air of historical charm.

In stark contrast, the neighborhood of Fatih holds a more conservative and traditional ambiance. Deeply rooted in the Islamic culture, Fatih's streets are adorned with mosques, bustling bazaars, and ornate buildings. The district provides an authentic glimpse into the day-to-day lives of many Istanbulites, far removed from the tourist-heavy attractions.

Crossing over to the Asian side of the city, Kadikoy emerges as a vibrant cultural hub. Known for its youthful and energetic spirit, Kadikoy's markets, lively bars, and eclectic dining scene make it a favorite among locals and visitors alike. The neighborhood exudes a bohemian charm, with its streets filled with colorful murals and bustling with artistic activity.

Uskudar, also on the Asian side, presents a starkly different yet equally captivating experience. Its waterfront promenade offers stunning views of the Bosphorus and the European side of the city.

The area is dotted with historic mosques and traditional tea houses, capturing a more relaxed and familial aspect of Istanbul.

Each neighborhood in Istanbul, Turkey contributes to the city's dynamic identity. From the historical grandeur of Sultanahmet to the modern vibrancy of Kadikoy, and the conservative essence of Fatih to the artistic allure of Karakoy, Istanbul's diverse districts collectively narrate the story of a city that is as multifaceted as it is timeless.Istanbul, Turkey, a city that spans two continents, is a vibrant mosaic of history, culture, and modernity. Each of its districts has its own unique charm, prompting both admiration and critique from locals and visitors alike. Evaluating the pros and cons of its various areas can provide valuable insights for those considering a visit or stay.

The Historic Peninsula, or Sultanahmet, is perhaps the most iconic part of Istanbul. It houses landmarks like the Hagia Sophia, Blue Mosque, and Topkapi Palace, making it a hub for history enthusiasts. The pros of Sultanahmet include its rich cultural heritage, picturesque views, and proximity to major tourist attractions. However, the area can be overwhelmingly crowded, particularly during peak tourist seasons. Additionally, the high concentration of tourist-oriented businesses sometimes overshadows the genuine local culture.

Beyoglu, encompassing neighborhoods like Taksim and Istiklal Street, is the heart of modern Istanbul. This area offers a bustling nightlife, a variety of restaurants, and an array of shopping options. The pros of Beyoglu are its vibrant atmosphere, abundant entertainment choices, and convenient access to public transport. On the downside, Beyoglu can be noisy and chaotic, with traffic congestion and high living costs posing significant challenges.

The Asian side of Istanbul, particularly districts like Kadikoy and Uskudar, offers a different flavor of the city. Kadikoy, with its lively markets and trendy cafes, is a favorite among the younger crowd. Uskudar offers stunning views of the Bosphorus and historical sites. The pros of the Asian side include a more relaxed, suburban feel, relatively lower living costs, and beautiful waterfront areas. However, some might find it less dynamic compared to the European side, and daily commutes to the European side can be time-consuming.

Besiktas, another popular district, is known for its bustling fish market, sports culture, and vibrant street life. The pros of Besiktas include its lively community, excellent food scene, and scenic Bosphorus views. However, its popularity leads to heavy traffic and higher living expenses. The constant buzz might not be suitable for those seeking tranquility.

Finally, districts like Nisantasi and Etiler represent the upscale side of Istanbul. These areas offer luxurious shopping, fine dining, and a high standard of living. The pros include excellent amenities, safety, and a clean environment. On the flip side, the cost of living is significantly higher, and the exclusivity might not appeal to everyone.

In conclusion, each area of Istanbul, Turkey, has its own distinct set of advantages and disadvantages. Whether one is drawn to the historical allure of Sultanahmet, the modern vibrancy of Beyoglu, the relaxed ambiance of the Asian side, the bustling life of Besiktas, or the upscale appeal of Nisantasi and Etiler, Istanbul offers a diverse tapestry that caters to a wide range of preferences and lifestyles. Understanding these nuances can help individuals make informed decisions about which district best suits their needs and desires.Istanbul, Turkey, is a mesmerising city where East meets West, history mingles with modernity, and vibrant markets stand alongside serene mosques. For budget-conscious travellers, Istanbul offers a plethora of options that allow you to explore its wonders without breaking the bank.

Accommodation is a crucial consideration, and in Istanbul, budget travellers have numerous choices. Hostels are scattered throughout the city, particularly in the Sultanahmet and Beyoglu districts. These hostels provide dormitory-style lodging and often include perks such as free breakfast, Wi-Fi, and activities to meet fellow travellers. For those who prefer a bit more privacy, guesthouses and budget hotels are available, offering basic yet comfortable accommodations at reasonable prices.

Istanbul's culinary scene is both delicious and affordable. Street food is ubiquitous and satisfying, with options like simit, a type of sesame-encrusted bread, available for a fraction of the price of a sit-down meal. Budget eateries serve hearty portions of local favourites like kebabs, mezes, and the deliciously sweet baklava. Many restaurants offer set menus or lunchtime specials, providing an opportunity to sample a variety of dishes without emptying your wallet.

Transportation around the city is efficient and inexpensive. Visitors can purchase an Istanbulkart, a reloadable card that grants access to trams, buses, funiculars, and ferries. The extensive public transit system ensures that you can traverse the city for a minimal cost. Walking is another excellent way to explore, especially in areas rich with historical landmarks and charming streets.

Istanbul is rich in history and culture, much of which can be experienced for free or at a low cost. The city's many mosques, such as the iconic Blue Mosque and the impressive Suleymaniye Mosque, are open to visitors without charge. Wandering through the bustling Grand Bazaar or the aromatic Spice Bazaar can be an enriching experience without necessitating significant spending. For a small fee, you can visit the Hagia Sophia Museum, Topkapi Palace, or the Basilica Cistern, each offering a glimpse into Turkey's storied past.

Parks and public spaces provide an additional layer of enjoyment. Take a leisurely stroll through Gulhane Park or relax by the Bosphorus waterfront while marvelling at views of both Asia and Europe. The Princes' Islands, a short and inexpensive ferry ride away, offer a peaceful escape from the city's hustle and bustle.

In summary, Istanbul, Turkey, is a destination where budget travellers can truly experience the richness of its culture, cuisine, and history. With careful planning and a spirit of adventure, it is entirely possible to enjoy the treasures of this vibrant city without spending a fortune.Istanbul, Turkey, is a city that beautifully combines history and modernity. For travelers who desire comfort without delving into the realm of luxury, mid-range choices in Istanbul offer an excellent balance of quality and affordability. Centrally located in various parts of the city, these options provide convenient access to key attractions while ensuring a pleasant stay.

In the heart of Sultanahmet, several mid-range hotels offer guests the chance to wake up overlooking iconic landmarks such as the Hagia Sophia and the Blue Mosque. These establishments often boast charming architecture that reflects the rich cultural heritage of the area, and many provide complimentary breakfasts to start the day with a taste of local flavors. The nearby streets are lined with cafes and shops where visitors can experience the vibrant atmosphere of Istanbul without stretching their budget too thin.

Another popular area for mid-range accommodations is Beyoglu, known for its lively nightlife and artistic vibe. Here, boutique hotels and well-appointed guesthouses offer modern amenities paired with a personalized touch. Staying in Beyoglu places visitors within walking distance of Istiklal Street, a bustling pedestrian thoroughfare brimming with shops, restaurants, and cultural venues. The district's blend of old-world charm and contemporary energy creates a unique experience for those looking to explore Istanbul's dynamic character.

Karakoy, situated along the waterfront, is another neighborhood offering appealing mid-range choices. This district seamlessly marries the historic with the trendy, featuring restored buildings that house stylish hotels. Guests can enjoy stunning views of the Bosphorus while being close to the Galata Tower and the vibrant Karakoy pier. The area is a gastronomic haven, with numerous eateries serving everything from traditional Turkish dishes to international cuisine, perfect for food lovers on a mid-range budget.

Furthermore, the Asian side of Istanbul, particularly the Kadikoy district, presents an array of mid-range options that offer a different perspective of the city. Kadikoy is known for its relaxed, local atmosphere, and staying here provides an escape from the more tourist-heavy European side. Well-regarded mid-range hotels and cozy bed-and-breakfasts abound, allowing guests to explore the historic Haydarpasa Train Station and the bustling Kadikoy Market.

Across all these neighborhoods, the common thread among mid-range accommodations in Istanbul is their commitment to delivering value. Whether through exceptional service, prime locations, or appealing amenities, these lodgings ensure a memorable visit without unnecessary extravagance. Mid-range choices in Istanbul encapsulate the essence of the city—welcoming, diverse, and full of life—making them an ideal option for travelers seeking an authentic and comfortable experience.Luxury Stays in Istanbul, Turkey

Istanbul, Turkey, a city where East meets West, offers a plethora of luxury stays that seamlessly blend opulence with history. As Turkey's largest city and its cultural and economic hub, Istanbul is home to an array of five-star hotels and high-end accommodations, each providing a unique experience rooted in the city's rich heritage and vibrant modern life.

One of the most iconic luxury stays in Istanbul is the Ciragan Palace Kempinski. This former Ottoman palace, majestically situated by the Bosphorus strait, offers guests an experience of regal splendor. The palatial architecture, expansive landscaped gardens, and stunning waterfront views make the Ciragan Palace an epitome of luxury. Guests can indulge in world-class amenities, including gourmet dining, a lavish spa, and impeccably designed rooms and suites that reflect the grandeur of the Ottoman era.

Another notable destination for opulent accommodations is the Four Seasons Hotel Istanbul at Sultanahmet. Located in the heart of the historic district, this lavish hotel is set in a century-old neoclassical prison. It provides an intimate and exclusive retreat within walking distance of renowned landmarks like the Hagia Sophia and the Blue

Mosque. The property masterfully combines modern comforts with historical charm, where guests can unwind in the serene courtyard garden or enjoy a panoramic view of the city's historical skyline from the rooftop terrace.

For those seeking a contemporary luxury experience, the Raffles Istanbul at Zorlu Center is a perfect choice. This modern marvel is a sanctuary of refined elegance, featuring spacious rooms with floor-to-ceiling windows that offer breathtaking views of the Bosphorus and the cityscape. The hotel is renowned for its exceptional service, sophisticated dining options, and a world-class spa that combines traditional Turkish treatments with modern wellness practices.

The St. Regis Istanbul, located in the upscale Nisantasi district, is another example of luxurious accommodation. Known for its timeless elegance and bespoke service, the St. Regis provides an intimate and sophisticated ambiance. The hotel's stylish interiors, curated art collection, and personalized butler service set a new standard for luxury.

Lastly, the Shangri-La Bosphorus offers a serene and elegant refuge along the shores of the Bosphorus. This hotel stands out for its stunning décor, which blends Asian hospitality with Turkish influences. Guests can relax in lavish rooms and suites that offer sweeping views of the strait, dine at the renowned Shang Palace, or rejuvenate in the exquisite CHI, The Spa.

In Istanbul, luxury is not just about extravagant accommodations but also about immersing oneself in the city's unique blend of cultures, rich history, and breathtaking scenery. Each of these luxury stays not only promises an opulent experience but also allows guests to connect with the captivating essence of Istanbul. Whether it's the palatial grandeur of the Ciragan Palace, the historical charm of the Four Seasons at Sultanahmet, the modern elegance of Raffles, the timeless sophistication of St. Regis, or the serene opulence of Shangri-La,

Istanbul's luxury stays are sure to leave an indelible impression on every traveler.\

Chapter 5: Unveiling Istanbul's Charms

Istanbul, Turkey's largest city, is a fascinating tapestry of history, culture, and architectural grandeur. As a city that straddles two continents, Europe and Asia, Istanbul has been a significant crossroads of civilizations, serving as a bridge between the East and the West. Among its many attractions, some of the most iconic landmarks stand as testaments to its rich and diverse heritage.

One of the most renowned landmarks in Istanbul is the Hagia Sophia. Originally constructed as a cathedral in 537 AD by the Byzantine Emperor Justinian I, it was later converted into a mosque after the Ottoman conquest of Constantinople in 1453, and then into a museum in the 20th century. The Hagia Sophia is celebrated for its massive dome, stunning mosaics, and its remarkable history, reflecting the city's changing religious and cultural landscapes.

Adjacent to the Hagia Sophia is another architectural marvel, the Blue Mosque. Officially known as the Sultan Ahmed Mosque, it was built in the early 17th century during the rule of Ahmed I. The mosque is named after the blue tiles that adorn its interior walls and is known for its six minarets, an unusual feature for a mosque at the time of its construction. The structure beautifully blends classical Islamic architecture with Byzantine elements taken from the neighboring Hagia Sophia.

Topkapi Palace, once the main residence and administrative headquarters of the Ottoman sultans, is another major landmark. This sprawling complex, which was constructed in the 15th century, now serves as a museum showcasing a rich collection of Ottoman artifacts, including imperial treasures, religious relics, and exquisite examples of Islamic art. The palace's lavish courtyards, lush gardens, and opulent rooms provide insight into the grandeur and intrigue of the Ottoman Empire.

Just a short distance from these landmarks is the Basilica Cistern, an underground marvel built by the Byzantine Emperor Justinian I. This colossal subterranean structure was designed to store water for the city and features hundreds of ancient columns, including the famous Medusa heads. The eerie, atmospheric setting of the cistern has made it a popular attraction and a frequent site for cultural events and film shoots.

The Galata Tower offers another perspective on the city. Dating back to the 14th century, this medieval stone tower provides panoramic views of Istanbul from its observation deck. Originally built by the Genoese, the tower has served various purposes throughout its history, from a watchtower to a fire tower, and now stands as a symbol of the city.

Finally, the Grand Bazaar, one of the world's oldest and largest covered markets, offers a vibrant and bustling experience of Istanbul's commercial heart. Established in the 15th century, the market boasts over 4,000 shops selling everything from spices to jewelry, textiles to ceramics. It is a labyrinth of colors, sounds, and scents, capturing the essence of Istanbul's dynamic and diverse culture.

Each of these landmarks tells a part of Istanbul's long and complex story. They reflect the city's status as a melting pot of different cultures and epochs, making Istanbul not just a city, but a living museum of human history.Istanbul, Turkey is a city teeming with historical significance and cultural heritage, standing at the crossroads of Europe and Asia. This unique positioning has made Istanbul a rich tapestry of history, blending influences from both continents over millennia. As one of the world's oldest continuously inhabited cities, Istanbul boasts a plethora of historical sites that offer a glimpse into its storied past.

One of the most iconic landmarks in Istanbul is the Hagia Sophia. Originally constructed as a cathedral in A.D. 537 during the reign of the Byzantine Emperor Justinian I, it stood as the world's largest cathedral for nearly a thousand years. Later, it was converted into a mosque following the Ottoman conquest in 1453, and today, it functions as a museum. The Hagia Sophia is renowned for its massive dome, intricate mosaics, and a stunning blend of Christian and Islamic architectural elements.

Another historical marvel is the Topkapi Palace, which served as the primary residence and administrative headquarters of the Ottoman sultans for nearly 400 years. Built in the 15th century by Sultan Mehmed II, the palace is now a museum complex that houses an exquisite collection of artifacts, including imperial garments, weapons, and sacred Islamic relics. Visitors are often mesmerized by the opulence of the palace's architecture, its lush courtyards, and the panoramic views it offers of the Bosphorus Strait.

The Blue Mosque, or Sultan Ahmed Mosque, is another architectural jewel of Istanbul. Completed in 1616, it is known for its six minarets and its cascading domes that create an imposing silhouette on the city's skyline. The interior of the mosque is adorned with more than 20,000 handmade Iznik tiles in blue hues, which is how it earned its popular name. The mosque is not only a place of worship but also a testament to the architectural grandeur of the Ottoman Empire.

The Basilica Cistern, located just a few steps from the Hagia Sophia, is an underground marvel built in the 6th century during the reign of Emperor Justinian I. This vast subterranean reservoir once supplied water to the Great Palace of Constantinople and other buildings. Its 336 marble columns, standing amongst the eerie reflections in the water below, create a surreal and captivating atmosphere that continues to draw visitors.

The historical sites of Istanbul would not be complete without mentioning the Grand Bazaar, one of the largest and oldest covered markets in the world. Established in the 15th century, the Grand Bazaar sprawls over 60 streets and encompasses more than 4,000 shops. It is a vibrant maze where visitors can find everything from traditional Turkish carpets and ceramics to spices and jewelry, offering an experience that is as much about immersing oneself in the local culture as it is about shopping.

These landmarks, among many others, make Istanbul a city where history is not just preserved, but lived every day. Walking through Istanbul is like traversing through time, with each site narrating its own unique chapter of a city that has been a witness to countless empires, cultures, and epochs. This convergence of past and present makes Istanbul a truly mesmerizing destination for history enthusiasts and casual visitors alike.Must-See Museums in Istanbul, Turkey

Istanbul, Turkey is a city that gracefully bridges the past and the present, offering an exquisite blend of history and modernity. Among its many attractions, the museums stand out as repositories of rich heritage, culture, and art. Visitors to the city will find an array of must-see museums that vividly narrate the story of not just Istanbul, but of civilizations that have intersected here over the centuries.

The Hagia Sophia Museum is arguably the most iconic of Istanbul's cultural landmarks. Originally constructed in 537 AD as a cathedral, it was later converted into a mosque and now functions as a museum. The stunning architectural feat melds Byzantine and Ottoman influences, housing intricate mosaics, massive domes, and minarets that evoke both splendor and spiritualism.

Another gem is the Topkapi Palace Museum, which was the primary residence of the Ottoman Sultans for almost 400 years. This sprawling complex comprises several buildings, courtyards, and gardens. Within its walls lies the hallowed Imperial Treasury, home to priceless artifacts such as the Topkapi Dagger and the Spoonmaker's Diamond. The Harem section, where the sultan's family lived, provides a fascinating glimpse into the secluded lives of the royals.

The Istanbul Archaeological Museums is another must-visit for history buffs. This complex of three museums - the Archaeological Museum, the Museum of the Ancient Orient, and the Museum of Islamic Art - houses over one million objects. Among its treasures are the Alexander Sarcophagus and the Kadesh Peace Treaty, both irreplaceable artifacts that offer glimpses into civilizations long past.

Located in the vibrant area of Beyoğlu, the Pera Museum offers a different flavor of cultural richness. Focusing extensively on Orientalist art, the museum exhibits works by both Turkish and international artists. Its collection includes classic paintings as well as unique objects such as Anatolian weights and measures, reflecting varied aspects of regional heritage.

The Istanbul Modern is the leading museum of contemporary art in the city. Situated along the Bosporus, it features works by groundbreaking Turkish artists alongside global contemporary pieces. The museum's dynamic exhibitions, educational programs, and film screenings make it a vital part of Istanbul's modern cultural landscape.

For an immersive and somewhat unconventional experience, the Rahmi M. Koç Museum is a treasure trove of industrial history. Situated on the picturesque shores of the Golden Horn, this museum showcases historical artifacts related to transport, industry, and communications. Highlights include a real submarine, vintage cars, and an extensive collection of model trains, making it a favorite among both children and adults.

Lastly, the Museum of Turkish and Islamic Arts, housed in the former palace of İbrahim Pasha, offers an intimate look at the artistic and cultural accomplishments of the Islamic world. From exquisitely detailed carpets to fine calligraphy and woodwork, the museum's comprehensive collection embodies the intricate beauty and profound depth of Islamic art.

In summary, the museums of Istanbul are more than just repositories of artifacts; they are vibrant windows into the soul of the city. Whether one is an avid historian, an art aficionado, or someone simply seeking to understand the diverse cultural tapestries of Turkey, these must-see museums provide invaluable insights and unforgettable experiences.Istanbul, Turkey, is a city that effortlessly bridges the past and the present, offering a tapestry of unique attractions that appeal to all types of travelers. Situated at the crossroads of Europe and Asia, this vibrant metropolis is filled with historical sites, cultural landmarks, and breathtaking natural beauty.

One of the most iconic attractions in Istanbul is the Hagia Sophia. Originally a cathedral, later a mosque, and now a museum, its architectural grandeur is a testament to the city's rich history. The vast dome and intricate mosaics of this monumental structure draw millions of visitors each year, eager to marvel at its splendor.

Another must-see destination is the Topkapi Palace, which served as the residence of Ottoman sultans for centuries. Here, visitors can wander through opulent rooms and lush courtyards, exploring an extensive collection of artifacts, including the famed Topkapi Dagger and the Prophet Muhammad's cloak.

The Blue Mosque, officially known as the Sultan Ahmed Mosque, is another highlight. Famous for its stunning blue tiles that line the interior walls, this majestic mosque is a functioning place of worship and a popular tourist attraction. Its six towering minarets and grand courtyard create an imposing yet serene atmosphere.

For those interested in experiencing the local culture, the Grand Bazaar offers a sensory overload of sights, sounds, and smells. One of the oldest and largest covered markets in the world, it boasts thousands of shops selling everything from intricate carpets to exquisite jewelry and aromatic spices. Haggling with vendors is an integral part of the shopping experience, adding to the bazaar's vibrant charm.

Venturing outside the historical peninsula, visitors can explore modern attractions such as the Istanbul Modern Art Museum, which showcases contemporary Turkish art, or take a leisurely stroll along Istiklal Avenue, a bustling pedestrian street lined with boutiques, cafes, and historical buildings.

Cruising on the Bosphorus is another unforgettable experience. This strait separates the European and Asian sides of Istanbul, offering panoramic views of palaces, fortresses, and the city's skyline. Travelers can choose from a variety of boat tours, from short rides to full-day excursions, all providing a unique perspective of the city's beauty.

A trip to Istanbul would be incomplete without indulging in its culinary delights. The city is a gastronomic paradise featuring everything from flavorful street food like simit and kestane to lavish Ottoman-inspired cuisine served in upscale restaurants.

In essence, Istanbul is a city where history and modernity coexist in perfect harmony. Its unique attractions make it an unforgettable destination for anyone seeking to explore a place rich in culture, history, and natural beauty.Local Favorites in Istanbul, Turkey

Istanbul, Turkey, a city that straddles two continents, is renowned for its rich cultural heritage and vibrant city life. From its historic landmarks to its bustling markets, Istanbul offers a plethora of local favorites that captivate both residents and visitors alike.

One of the most cherished local experiences is exploring the Grand Bazaar. With its labyrinthine alleys and over four thousand shops, the Grand Bazaar is one of the largest and oldest covered markets in the world. Here, you can find a diverse array of goods, from intricate jewelry and handmade ceramics to colorful textiles and aromatic spices. The bazaar is not just a shopping destination but a cultural experience where each turn reveals a new delight.

No visit to Istanbul would be complete without savoring the flavors of its diverse cuisine. The city's food scene is a melting pot of influences from the Ottoman Empire, Mediterranean, and Middle Eastern flavors. A local favorite is the balik ekmek, a simple yet delicious fish sandwich typically sold along the shores of the Bosphorus. Made with freshly grilled fish, onions, lettuce, and a squeeze of lemon juice, this sandwich is a mouthwatering treat. Another beloved dish is the iconic kebab, with numerous variations such as adana and doner, each offering its distinctive taste.

Istanbul is also famous for its traditional Turkish tea and coffee culture. The city is dotted with countless tea gardens and coffeehouses where locals gather for a moment of relaxation and conversation. Enjoying a cup of strong Turkish coffee, often accompanied by a piece of Turkish delight, is an essential part of the Istanbulite experience. Similarly, sipping on a glass of black tea served in tulip-shaped glasses is a time-honored custom.

For those with a penchant for history and architecture, Istanbul boasts some of the most stunning landmarks in the world. The Hagia Sophia, with its grand dome and intricate mosaics, stands as a testament to the city's Byzantine and Ottoman past. Similarly, the Blue Mosque, celebrated for its six minarets and exquisite Iznik tiles, never fails to leave visitors in awe. The serene Topkapi Palace, once the residence of Ottoman sultans, offers a glimpse into the opulent lifestyle of a bygone era.

Beyond its historic sites, Istanbul's neighborhoods each bring their own unique flavor to the city's tapestry. The bohemian district of Karakoy is a hub for artists and young creatives, filled with trendy cafes, art galleries, and boutique shops. In contrast, Balat displays a more traditional ambiance with its colorful houses and a myriad of small, family-run businesses.

In conclusion, Istanbul, Turkey is a city where history, culture, and modernity intertwine seamlessly. Its local favorites, whether they be culinary delights, historical landmarks, or vibrant neighborhoods, create an unforgettable experience. Istanbul is truly a city that never ceases to enchant and inspire all who visit.Walking Tours in Istanbul, Turkey

Istanbul, Turkey, a city that straddles two continents, offers an enchanting blend of history, culture, and architectural beauty. One of the best ways to experience the richness of this vibrant metropolis is through walking tours, allowing visitors to immerse themselves in the pulse of the city.

From the moment you set foot in Istanbul, the rhythm of daily life and the echoes of ancient times are palpable. The city is dotted with landmarks that tell the stories of empires and civilizations long past. A walking tour often begins in the heart of the old city, within the Sultanahmet District. Here, the towering minarets of the Sultan Ahmed Mosque, known as the Blue Mosque, pierce the sky. The interior, adorned with tens of thousands of blue Iznik tiles, provides a serene yet awe-inspiring experience.

Just a short stroll away lies the Hagia Sophia, a marvel of Byzantine architecture that has served as a cathedral, mosque, and now a museum. Its massive dome and intricate mosaics are testaments to the architectural ingenuity of ancient builders. Walking through its halls transports one back to a time when it served as the epicenter of Orthodox Christianity and later the Ottoman Empire.

Adjacent to the Hagia Sophia is the Topkapi Palace, once the primary residence of Ottoman sultans. Wandering through its courtyards, visitors can marvel at the opulence and grandeur of the empire's seat of power. The Harem section, in particular, evokes intrigue and wonder, offering glimpses into the private lives of the sultans and their families.

Leaving the historical peninsula, a walking tour might take you across the Galata Bridge to the bustling Beyoglu District. The Istiklal Avenue, a long and lively pedestrian street, is a hub of modern Istanbul. With its array of shops, cafes, and historic arcades, it is a place where the old meets the new. The iconic Galata Tower offers panoramic views of the cityscape and is a must-visit for anyone wishing to understand the city's layout from above.

For those interested in the more tranquil side of Istanbul, a walk along the Bosphorus strait is ideal. The waterfront promenade provides stunning views of both the European and Asian shores. The serene atmosphere is punctuated by the sight of ferries and ships navigating the strait, demonstrating Istanbul's role as a crossroads of cultures and trade.

No walking tour in Istanbul would be complete without a visit to the Grand Bazaar. With its labyrinthine network of stalls and shops, it is one of the largest and oldest covered markets in the world. Exploring its alleys reveals a treasure trove of goods, from spices and textiles to jewelry and ceramics. The bazaar's vibrant energy is a reflection of the city's bustling commercial life.

In conclusion, walking tours offer an intimate and engaging way to explore Istanbul. The city's layered history, architectural wonders, and lively streetscape come alive on foot, providing a sensory-rich experience that leaves an indelible mark on those who traverse its paths. Whether one is a history buff, a culture enthusiast, or simply a curious traveler, Istanbul's walking tours reveal the essence of a city that has been a crossroads of civilizations for millennia.Istanbul, Turkey, is a city of immense historical depth, rich cultural heritage, and unparalleled vibrancy. One of the best ways to immerse oneself in the unique essence of this metropolis is through specialty tours, each offering a lens into different facets of the city. Specialty tours in Istanbul provide both visitors and locals an opportunity to explore the city beyond its iconic landmarks, diving deep into its culinary wonders, artistic treasures, and hidden gems.

Food enthusiasts will find culinary tours particularly enthralling. Istanbul is a melting pot of flavors, blending influences from the Middle East, Europe, and Asia. Guided by knowledgeable locals, these tours take participants through bustling markets like the Grand Bazaar and Spice Bazaar, where the air is laden with the aroma of exotic spices. Stops at traditional eateries offer samples of mouthwatering delicacies such as simit, a circular bread encrusted with sesame seeds, or baklava, a sweet pastry dripping with honey. Discovering the intricacies of Turkish tea and coffee culture adds even more depth to this sensory journey.

For history buffs, Istanbul's past unfolds through specialty tours that focus on its Byzantine and Ottoman heritage. Walking through the ancient ruins of the Hippodrome transports you to the days of chariot races and grand public events. Visits to the Hagia Sophia and Topkapi Palace reveal the city's architectural magnificence and storied past. With expert guides providing rich commentary, these tours transform the way one perceives the structures that have stood the test of time.

Art and culture tours also offer a captivating glimpse into Istanbul's vibrant creative scene. These tours often include visits to contemporary galleries, artist ateliers, and cultural hubs that showcase modern Turkish art and design. Exploring neighborhoods like Karakoy and Balat, known for their bohemian flair and vibrant street art, gives participants a chance to see the city's creative spirit in full bloom.

Moreover, themed tours exploring the Bosphorus Strait provide an exceptional perspective of Istanbul's landscape. Cruising along the Bosphorus, which separates Europe and Asia, participants witness the stunning beauty of the city's skyline dotted with minarets and historical mansions. The serene waters offer a peaceful contrast to the energetic pulse of the city.

For those seeking something off the beaten path, Istanbul's specialty tours include explorations of its underground cisterns, hidden neighborhoods, and even historical hammams, or Turkish baths. These unique experiences allow visitors to peel back the layers of the city, revealing stories that are not always apparent at first glance.

In essence, specialty tours in Istanbul cater to a variety of interests, making the city accessible and engaging for diverse audiences. Whether one is drawn to food, history, art, or simply the allure of discovering something new, these tours offer a richly textured experience that highlights Istanbul's multifaceted charm. Through the knowledge and passion of experienced guides, participants gain not only insight but also a deeper appreciation for the timeless beauty of Istanbul, Turkey.Popular Experiences in Istanbul, Turkey

Istanbul, Turkey, offers a blend of history, culture, and modernity, providing visitors with a plethora of memorable experiences. As a city that bridges two continents, Europe and Asia, it boasts an eclectic mix of architectural marvels, bustling bazaars, and scenic landscapes. One of the most iconic experiences in Istanbul is visiting the Hagia Sophia. Originally a cathedral, later a mosque, and now a museum, its massive dome and stunning mosaics are a testament to Byzantine and Ottoman artistry.

Another must-see is the Topkapi Palace. Once the residence of Ottoman sultans, this sprawling complex offers a glimpse into the opulence of the empire with its lavish rooms, courtyards, and breathtaking views over the Bosphorus. Close by, the Blue Mosque stands as a marvel of Ottoman architecture, with its cascading domes and six minarets. The interior, adorned with tens of thousands of blue Iznik tiles, creates an atmosphere of serene beauty.

For those who love shopping and local experiences, the Grand Bazaar is a labyrinth of more than 4,000 shops offering everything from jewelry to spices. It is one of the oldest and largest covered markets in the world, where haggling is expected and part of the fun. Similarly, the Spice Bazaar provides a sensory delight with its array of colorful spices, dried fruits, and Turkish delights.

No visit to Istanbul is complete without a Bosphorus cruise. This waterway not only separates Europe and Asia but also offers spectacular views of the city's skyline, dotted with grand palaces, historic fortresses, and modern structures. The vibrant neighborhoods of Karakoy and Kadikoy, situated on the European and Asian sides respectively, provide a taste of contemporary Istanbul with their trendy cafes, art galleries, and bustling markets.

Istanbul's rich culinary scene is another highlight. From savoring kebabs and mezze in traditional Turkish restaurants to enjoying street food like simit and roasted chestnuts, the city caters to all palates. Do not miss the chance to indulge in a leisurely Turkish breakfast, featuring an assortment of cheeses, olives, jams, and freshly baked bread, served with the quintessential Turkish tea.

Finally, the public baths or hammams offer a quintessential Istanbul experience that combines relaxation and cultural immersion. Stepping into a historic hammam, with its marble interiors and elaborate bathing rituals, transports visitors to a time-honored tradition of cleansing and rejuvenation.

In conclusion, Istanbul, Turkey, is a city of endless fascination and diverse experiences. Whether you are admiring its historical architecture, exploring its lively bazaars, cruising along the Bosphorus, or indulging in its culinary delights, this city has something to captivate every visitor.

Chapter 6: Culinary Delights of Istanbul

Istanbul, Turkey, stands at the crossroads of Europe and Asia, and its food culture is a testament to this unique geographical blend. The local cuisine is a vibrant mosaic that reflects the city's rich history, cultural diversity, and the bounty of its surrounding seas and lands. In Istanbul, food is more than mere sustenance; it is a way of life, a social glue that brings people together, and a vital aspect of the city's identity.

At the heart of Istanbul's food culture is its bustling markets, with the most famous being the Grand Bazaar and the Spice Bazaar. Here, locals and tourists alike can explore an array of spices, teas, dried fruits, nuts, and sweets that provide the foundation for many traditional dishes. The aroma of freshly ground coffee and the sight of colorful sweets, like Turkish delight, create an intoxicating sensory experience that is quintessentially Istanbul.

Street food is an integral part of Istanbul's culinary scene, offering both convenience and authentic flavors. Simit, a sesame-covered bread ring, is a popular snack that can be found at almost every street corner. Another beloved street food is balik ekmek, a fish sandwich that features fresh fish, usually mackerel, grilled to perfection and served with simple garnishes inside a crusty roll. These quick bites capture the essence of Istanbul's food culture: simple, fresh, and deeply satisfying.

A visit to Istanbul would be incomplete without indulging in its traditional dishes. Breakfast, or kahvalti, often includes a spread of olives, cheese, tomatoes, cucumbers, and fresh bread, complemented by sweet and savory spreads. The meal is not rushed and serves as a perfect start to the day. For lunch or dinner, kebabs and mezes are popular choices. Kebabs come in various styles, from the skewered shish kebab to the spiced minced meat of adana kebab. Mezes, which are small appetizer plates, might include dishes like hummus, baba ghanoush, and dolmas, offering a flavorful and communal dining experience.

Seafood is also a crucial part of Istanbul's diet, thanks to the city's proximity to the Bosphorus Strait. Fresh fish from the Bosphorus and the Marmara Sea is a staple, often enjoyed grilled or baked. Delicacies like stuffed mussels and calamari are also widely appreciated.

Istanbul's dessert scene is equally impressive, with baklava being the star. Layers of thin phyllo dough, butter, nuts, and sweet syrup create a delicacy that is both crunchy and melt-in-your-mouth soft. Other popular sweets include kunefe, a cheese pastry soaked in syrup, and sutlac, a creamy rice pudding often topped with cinnamon or nuts.

Tea and coffee hold special places in Istanbul's food culture. Turkish tea is typically strong and served in tulip-shaped glasses, while Turkish coffee is thick, rich, and often enjoyed slowly while socializing. Both beverages are more than drinks; they are part of the social fabric of Istanbul.

In summary, Istanbul's local food culture is a rich tapestry woven with history, tradition, and a blend of influences from both the East and West. It emphasizes fresh ingredients, communal dining, and an appreciation for simple yet profound flavors. For anyone visiting Istanbul, immersing themselves in the city's culinary offerings is an essential part of the experience, offering a deliciously deep dive into the soul of this captivating city.Istanbul, Turkey is a city where the confluence of tradition and modernity is both striking and seamless. This historic metropolis straddles two continents, Europe and Asia, which has imbued it with a rich tapestry of cultural influences. As one of the most significant cities in world history, Istanbul has been the capital of three great empires: the Roman, Byzantine, and Ottoman. These layers of history are evident in its landmarks, culinary traditions, and daily life.

Influences from different eras and empires create a unique cultural mosaic in Istanbul. The Byzantine heritage is most prominent in the form of the Hagia Sophia, originally built as an Orthodox basilica and later converted into a mosque, and now serving as a museum. This architectural wonder stands as a testament to the citys deep-rooted Christian history, even as it has mostly embraced Islam. Nearby stands the Blue Mosque, an emblem of Ottoman artistry, with its intricate tile work and towering minarets. The juxtaposition of these two iconic structures encapsulates the blend of old and new, East and West, sacred and secular.

The culinary landscape of Istanbul further reflects this multifaceted heritage. Meandering through the city's vibrant streets, one can sample a wide array of cuisines that have been influenced by various regions and peoples over centuries. From the bustling markets of the Grand Bazaar and Spice Bazaar, offering Turkish delight, dried fruits, and exotic spices, to the ubiquitous street vendors selling simit and chestnuts, to the fine dining establishments along the Bosphorus, every meal tells a story. Traditional Turkish dishes such as kebabs, mezes, and baklava have been perfected and adapted over generations, showcasing the city's ability to honor its past while embracing new trends and techniques.

Traditions in Istanbul are not confined to its buildings and food; they are alive in its festivals, music, and daily rituals. The city celebrates a diverse array of religious and cultural events, from the somber observance of Ramadan to the joyous festivities of the Istanbul International Music Festival. The call to prayer from countless mosques creates a spiritual rhythm to daily life, interspersed with the hustle and bustle of modern living.

Modern influences have also found their place in Istanbul, creating a dynamic urban environment. Neighborhoods such as Beyoglu and Kadikoy are hubs for contemporary arts, music, and fashion, where young creatives push the boundaries while still paying homage to their cultural roots. Art galleries, modern cafes, and music venues provide the city with a vibrant, youthful energy that exists in harmony with its ancient soul.

Istanbul's ability to harmonize myriad influences while maintaining its unique traditions makes it a fascinating city that never ceases to amaze visitors and residents alike. It is a place where history is palpably present and the future is eagerly anticipated, a testament to the enduring and evolving spirit of this remarkable city.Istanbul, Turkey, a city that straddles both Europe and Asia, is a melting pot of cultures and cuisines. The vibrant tapestry of its history is reflected in its food, with signature dishes that showcase the fusion of flavors and traditions. The city's culinary landscape offers a mosaic of tastes, inviting locals and visitors alike to indulge in its gastronomic heritage.

One cannot mention Istanbul without giving due reverence to the iconic kebabs. The city is renowned for its diverse kebab offerings, each presenting a unique blend of spices and cooking methods. From the succulent lamb kebabs, known as kuzu sis, to the flavorful doner kebabs where thin slices of meat are brushed with rich sauces, Istanbul's kebabs are a testament to the city's mastery in grilling and seasoning.

Another staple in Istanbul's cuisine is the beloved meze platter. Served as an appetizer or even as a main course, the meze includes small, savory dishes that entice the palate. Spread with an assortment of fresh bread, the platter typically features items such as hummus, stuffed grape leaves, and the delectable muhammara, a tangy red pepper dip. Each bite brings an explosion of diverse flavors, making the meze an integral part of the Istanbul dining experience.

Further complementing the city's culinary scene are the famous pide and lahmacun, often referred to as Turkish pizza. The pide comes with a variety of toppings, from minced meat to spinach and cheese, enclosed within a boat-shaped flatbread. Lahmacun, on the other hand, is a thinner, round flatbread topped with minced meat, onions, tomatoes, and herbs, rolled up and eaten like a wrap. Both dishes are adored for their simplicity and taste, reflecting the comfort food culture of Istanbul.

No discussion of Istanbul's cuisine would be complete without mentioning baklava, the sweet pastry that has captured the hearts of many. Layered with thin sheets of phyllo dough, filled with nuts, and soaked in syrup, baklava is a dessert that embodies the richness of Turkish sweets. Another popular dessert is the kadayif, shredded pastry dough also filled with nuts and sweetened with syrup, offering a different yet equally enchanting texture compared to baklava.

Istanbul's culinary delights do not end here. The city is also known for its array of street food, such as simit, a sesame-coated bread ring, and balik ekmek, a fish sandwich typically enjoyed by the bustling waterfront. Each street food item tells a story of tradition and modern-day life in Istanbul, ensuring that every visitor leaves with a taste of the city's vibrant food culture.

In conclusion, Istanbul, Turkey, is a city where culinary traditions meet innovation, offering an unforgettable journey through its signature dishes. From the vibrant flavors of kebabs and meze to the comforting taste of pide and lahmacun, to the decadent sweetness of baklava, Istanbul's cuisine captures the essence of this historic and dynamic city.Istanbul, Turkey, is a city that boasts an impressive array of regional specialties, all of which highlight its rich cultural tapestry and historical significance. This crossroads of civilizations has cultivated an unparalleled culinary heritage, one that has evolved over centuries and is influenced by a melange of Mediterranean, Middle Eastern, and Balkan traditions. Among the city's most celebrated dishes is the iconic kebab, a savory delight that comes in numerous forms such as the famous döner kebab, which consists of succulent, slow-cooked meat shaved from a vertical rotisserie and typically served wrapped in flatbread or as a sandwich with crisp, fresh vegetables.

Another quintessential Istanbul experience is indulging in meze, a splendid assortment of small plates that can encompass everything from hummus and baba ghanoush to grilled octopus and stuffed vine leaves. These dishes are often shared among friends and family, embodying the communal spirit that is at the heart of Turkish dining culture. Istanbul's regional specialties also include a wide range of seafood, thanks to its prime location along the Bosphorus Strait. Fresh fish like mackerel and sea bass are often grilled to perfection and served with simple yet delicious side dishes such as lemon wedges and fresh herbs.

The city is also renowned for its pastries and sweets, with baklava being perhaps the most famous. This decadent dessert, made of layers of paper-thin phyllo pastry filled with chopped nuts and sweetened with syrup or honey, is a testament to the city's historical affinity for intricate and luxurious flavors. Turkish delight, known locally as lokum, is another beloved confection, available in a variety of flavors and often infused with rosewater or citrus.

Of course, no discussion of Istanbul's culinary offerings would be complete without mentioning its coffee and tea culture. Turkish coffee, known for its intense flavor and thick, frothy texture, is a beverage steeped in tradition and is often enjoyed leisurely in the city's many charming cafés. Similarly, Turkish tea, or çay, is a staple of daily life, served in distinctive tulip-shaped glasses and usually accompanied by a small cube of sugar.

In summary, Istanbul's regional specialties offer a tantalizing glimpse into its rich and diverse heritage. From savory kebabs and delightful meze to exquisite pastries and traditional beverages, the city's culinary offerings are a testament to its vibrant history and the myriad of cultures that have shaped it. Whether indulging in a hearty meal or savoring a sweet treat, one can truly taste the essence of Istanbul in every bite.Istanbul, Turkey is a city that brims with fascinating diversity, where the grandeur of the past coexists harmoniously with vibrant contemporary life. It is a destination that caters to a multitude of interests, with each visitor finding something uniquely appealing. Here are some top picks by category to help guide you through this mesmerizing city.

For history enthusiasts, Istanbul is nothing short of a treasure trove. The Hagia Sophia stands as a testament to the city's rich historical tapestry, having served as a church, a mosque, and now a museum. Its awe-inspiring dome and intricate mosaics captivate millions of visitors each year. The Topkapi Palace, once the opulent home of Ottoman sultans, offers a glimpse into the extravagance and complexity of Ottoman court life. Do not miss the Basilica Cistern, an ancient underground water reservoir that epitomizes the engineering prowess of the Byzantine Empire.

Art and culture aficionados will find Istanbul's creative scene incredibly rewarding. The Istanbul Modern Museum showcases contemporary Turkish art in a variety of media, from painting to photography. For a more traditional experience, the Turkish and Islamic Arts Museum houses a stunning collection of calligraphy, tiles, and carpets. Small art galleries scattered throughout neighborhoods like Karakoy and Galata offer intimate looks at the burgeoning local art scene.

Istanbul's culinary landscape is as dynamic as its history. Street food lovers must try the iconic doner kebab and the sweet, sticky baklava found in stalls and small shops around the city. For a more refined dining experience, Neolokal offers modern interpretations of traditional Anatolian cuisines while capitalizing on sustainable practices. The city's bazaars, particularly the Grand Bazaar and the Spice Bazaar, allow visitors to indulge in a sensory fiesta, with heaps of spices, teas, and sweets that paint a vibrant portrait of Turkish flavors.

Shopping in Istanbul can be a delightful adventure, from luxury boutiques in Nişantaşı to the eclectic shops of Arasta Bazaar. The Grand Bazaar features thousands of shops selling everything from kilim rugs to intricate gold jewelry, representing a shopping experience that is both ancient and enduring. Weekends offer bustling markets like the Saturday Market in Ferikoy, perfect for those seeking organic produce and vintage finds.

Nature and outdoor lovers will appreciate the Bosphorus strait, an iconic waterway that not only separates two continents but also serves as a point of serene beauty. Boat tours along the Bosphorus provide unparalleled views of the city's skyline, marked by minarets and domed structures. For a more immersive natural experience, the Belgrad Forest offers a verdant escape from urban hustle, with trails perfect for walking or cycling.

Nightlife in Istanbul is effervescent and varied. Beyoglu district is the epicenter of the city's nightlife, with Istiklal Street boasting a plethora of bars, clubs, and live music venues. For a sophisticated evening, sunset cocktails at Mikla Restaurant's rooftop bar offer panoramic views that are hard to beat. Traditional experiences can be cherished at meyhanes, where you can enjoy raki and meze while listening to live Turkish folk music.

In essence, Istanbul, Turkey is a city where every corner tells a story, and every experience enriches its narrative. Whether you are a history buff, an art lover, a foodie, a shopper, a nature enthusiast, or a night owl, Istanbul has something special to offer, making it an unmissable destination on the world map.Istanbul, Turkey, renowned for its rich tapestry of history, diverse culture, and delectable cuisine, offers a surprising array of vegetarian and vegan options that cater to the growing demand for plant-based diets. Despite traditionally being known for its meat-heavy dishes such as kebabs and döner, the city has evolved to embrace the global shift toward vegetarianism and veganism.

The city's vibrant food scene ensures that vegetarians and vegans can indulge in an array of flavorful and fulfilling dishes. Many of Istanbul's restaurants and cafes have adapted their menus to include a variety of plant-based options, allowing for a seamless dining experience. One of the most delightful aspects of Turkish cuisine is its inherent use of fresh vegetables, legumes, and grains, which naturally lend themselves to vegetarian and vegan dishes.

Traditional Turkish mezes, small appetizer dishes, often include flavorful options such as hummus, baba ganoush, stuffed grape leaves, and lentil balls. These dishes are typically made with fresh, wholesome ingredients and are a staple in many Turkish households. Additionally, vegetarian versions of traditional main courses, like vegetable kebabs and stuffed peppers with rice and herbs, are widely available and equally satisfying.

The city also boasts several dedicated vegetarian and vegan restaurants that are creative in their culinary approach, offering innovative takes on traditional and international dishes. Some of these restaurants have garnered popularity not only among vegetarians and vegans but also among omnivores seeking healthier and more sustainable food choices.

Moreover, local markets and street vendors often sell fresh fruits, vegetables, nuts, and seeds, providing ample options for individuals who prefer to prepare their own meals. Vegan-friendly bakeries and dessert shops have also become more common, offering delightful treats such as vegan baklava and dairy-free ice creams that allow everyone to experience the sweet side of Turkish cuisine.

In summary, Istanbul, Turkey, with its dynamic culinary landscape, holds an abundance of vegetarian and vegan options that cater to diverse dietary preferences. Whether dining out at a high-end restaurant, exploring traditional markets, or enjoying street food, those following a plant-based diet will find that the city's gastronomic offerings are both plentiful and delicious.Best Street Food Markets in Istanbul, Turkey

Istanbul, Turkey, a city that bridges two continents, is renowned for its rich history and vibrant culture. Among the city's many attractions, its street food markets stand out as a must-visit for any traveler. The street food scene in Istanbul offers a delicious introduction to Turkish culinary traditions and provides a unique way to experience the spirit of the city.

One of the most famous street food markets in Istanbul is the Kadikoy Market located on the Asian side of the city. This bustling market is a paradise for food lovers, offering an array of local delicacies. Here, visitors can savor simit, a sesame-crusted bread that is often compared to a bagel, or enjoy mussels stuffed with spicy rice. The market is also home to several traditional Turkish sweets such as lokum, known worldwide as Turkish Delight, and baklava, a sweet pastry made of layers of filo filled with nuts and soaked in honey.

Another iconic destination is the Balik Ekmek vendors near the Galata Bridge. Balik Ekmek, which translates to "fish sandwich," is a local favorite. Freshly grilled fish is placed in crusty bread with a handful of lettuce and onions, resulting in a simple yet delectable meal. Enjoying a Balik Ekmek while watching the boats on the Bosphorus is an experience that captures the essence of Istanbul's seafaring history.

For those looking to explore more traditional Turkish dishes, the Karakoy Gulluoglu is a classic venue. This market is particularly famous for its baklava, considered among the best in the city. Visitors can indulge in a variety of flavors, ranging from pistachio to walnut, all while sipping on Turkish tea. The meticulous preparation and use of high-quality ingredients make this a highlight for anyone with a sweet tooth.

The Spice Bazaar, or Misir Carsisi, also holds an important place in Istanbul's street food scene. Though it is primarily known for its vibrant array of spices, dried fruits, and nuts, visitors can also find street food vendors offering items like gozleme, a savory Turkish flatbread filled with spinach, cheese, or minced meat. The lively atmosphere and fragrant aromas make the Spice Bazaar a sensory delight.

Lastly, the Istiklal Street offers a more modern street food experience. Amidst the historical buildings and contemporary shops, visitors can find stalls selling doner kebabs, a Turkish staple made of meat cooked on a vertical rotisserie and served in bread or wrap. Additionally, one can sample kokorec, a dish made of seasoned and grilled lamb intestines, and roasted chestnuts from street vendors that line the pedestrian avenue.

Exploring the street food markets of Istanbul is more than just a culinary adventure; it is an immersion into the city's diverse heritage and vibrant way of life. Each market and its offerings reflect the rich tapestry of tastes, traditions, and tales that make Istanbul a truly magical place to visit. Whether you are a foodie, a culture enthusiast, or a curious traveler, the street food of Istanbul promises an unforgettable journey for your palate.Istanbul, Turkey, is a city where East meets West, and this fusion is profoundly reflected in its street food culture. The city's bustling streets are a paradise for food lovers, offering a multitude of flavors that are both exotic and comforting. Street food in Istanbul is not just about quick bites; it is an intrinsic part of the city's culture and daily life.

One of the most iconic street foods in Istanbul is simit. Often described as a Turkish bagel, this sesame-coated bread is a staple for many locals. Vendors with carts selling simit can be found at almost every corner, especially in the morning. Turks often enjoy simit with a cup of tea, making it a perfect breakfast or snack on the go.

Another must-try street food is balik ekmek, which translates to "fish sandwich." Freshly caught fish from the Bosphorus Strait, usually mackerel, is grilled and placed in a loaf of bread with lettuce, onions, and a squeeze of lemon. Balik ekmek is often sold near the Galata Bridge, where the sight and smell of grilling fish prepare your senses for an unforgettable culinary experience.

For meat lovers, doner kebab is a street food that cannot be missed. Thin slices of marinated meat, typically lamb, chicken, or beef, are cooked on a vertical rotisserie and served in a pita or flatbread with vegetables and sauces. The spices and slow-cooking method give the meat its distinctive and delectable flavor, making it a favorite among both locals and tourists.

One of Istanbul's most beloved sweet treats is baklava, but for a street food twist, the city offers lokma. These deep-fried dough balls are soaked in sweet syrup and sometimes sprinkled with cinnamon or sesame seeds. Crunchy on the outside and soft on the inside, lokma is a delightful snack that can be enjoyed at any time of day.

Of course, no visit to Istanbul would be complete without tasting some midye dolma, or stuffed mussels. These mussels are filled with a mixture of spiced rice, pine nuts, and occasionally currants, served with a wedge of lemon. Vendors often serve them straight from the shells, making it a delicious and satisfying street side snack.

In Istanbul, the street food scene is a testament to the city's rich culinary heritage and its ability to bring together diverse flavors and influences. Whether you are savoring a simple simit or indulging in the complex flavors of midye dolma, the street foods of Istanbul offer a unique and flavorful journey through this vibrant city.

Chapter 7: Istanbul: Cultural Heartbeat and Heritage

Istanbul, Turkey, is a city that seamlessly blends history with modernity, serving as a vibrant hub for artistic expression. The city boasts several major art institutions that are pivotal in showcasing Turkey's rich cultural heritage and contemporary artistic advancements. Among these esteemed establishments is the Istanbul Modern, Turkey's first modern art museum, which opened its doors in 2004. Located on the shores of the Bosphorus, the museum has played a critical role in providing a platform for both established and emerging Turkish and international artists. Its comprehensive collection includes works ranging from painting and sculpture to photography and new media.

Another cornerstone in Istanbul's art scene is the Pera Museum, founded by the Suna and Inan Kiraç Foundation in 2005. This museum is renowned for its diverse collection that spans several centuries and cultures. The Pera Museum is particularly famous for its Orientalist paintings, Anatolian weights and measures, and Kutahya tiles and ceramics. It frequently hosts temporary exhibitions and cultural events, fostering a dynamic environment for art enthusiasts.

Sakıp Sabancı Museum, situated in Emirgan along the Bosphorus, is another significant institution dedicated to both classical and contemporary art. It houses a notable collection of calligraphy, religious and state documents, paintings, and decorative arts. The museum's extensive garden and modern facilities provide an inspiring setting for art exhibitions, educational programs, and international collaborations.

For those with an interest in more experimental and contemporary works, Arter is an essential stop. Arter initially opened in 2010 and later moved to its new location in Dolapdere in 2019, significantly expanding its capacity. It presents a wide array of contemporary art exhibitions and is well-regarded for its commitment to pushing the boundaries of artistic creation and interpretation.

Furthermore, Istanbul Biennial is a major event that invites contemporary artists from around the world to create and display socially engaging artworks across various venues in the city. Organized by the Istanbul Foundation for Culture and Arts, the Biennial transforms the city into a sprawling canvas, encouraging public interaction with contemporary art in diverse urban settings.

These major art institutions, alongside numerous galleries, cultural centers, and historic sites, make Istanbul a thriving epicenter for art and culture. They not only preserve and celebrate Turkey's artistic legacy but also innovate and challenge the boundaries of modern creativity, ensuring that Istanbul remains a lively and influential player in the global art community.Istanbul, Turkey, a city brimming with history and culture, offers a plethora of specialty museums that captivate the hearts and minds of visitors. These institutions go beyond the traditional realms of art and archaeology, delving into unique facets of heritage that provide a deeper understanding of both Istanbul and its people.

One such gem is the Istanbul Modern, which stands as the citys first modern art museum. Facing the Bosphorus, this museum presents an extensive collection of contemporary Turkish artworks. It serves not only as a gallery space but also as a cultural hub, featuring film screenings, educational programs, and an engaging library. The modern architecture of the museum itself is a testament to the fusion of traditional and contemporary that defines Istanbul.

Another intriguing institution is the Museum of Innocence, inspired by the novel of the same name by Nobel Prize-winning author Orhan Pamuk. This innovative museum offers a tangible counterpart to the fictional story, featuring everyday objects that evoke the novel's 1970s Istanbul setting. Visitors find themselves immersed in the narrative, where artifacts are carefully curated to reflect the poignant and intricate details of love and memory. This museum blurs the line between fact and fiction, creating a unique narrative experience.

For those fascinated by the macabre, the Ural Ataman Classic Car Museum provides an extensive collection of vintage automobiles. Car enthusiasts and history buffs will find themselves captivated by the meticulously restored vehicles, which range from early 20th-century models to post-war classics. Each car tells a story of its era, reflecting the technological advancements and cultural shifts that have influenced automotive design over the decades.

The Rahmi M. Koç Museum, dedicated to the history of transport, industry, and communications, offers another specialized experience. Housed in a historic dockyard, this museum features a vast array of exhibits, including steam engines, submarines, and even a Boeing 747 cockpit. The hands-on displays and interactive exhibits make it a particularly engaging destination for families and technology enthusiasts alike.

Lastly, the Istanbul Toy Museum provides a whimsical journey through history via the lens of childhood. Founded by poet and novelist Sunay Akin, the museum houses thousands of toys from around the world, some dating back to the 19th century. Each exhibit is carefully designed to evoke a sense of nostalgia and wonder, showcasing the cultural and societal changes reflected in these playful artifacts.

These specialty museums reveal the diverse interests and rich history of Istanbul, offering visitors unique insights into both the ancient and modern worlds that coexist within this dynamic city. Through their carefully curated exhibits, these institutions not only preserve the past but also inspire and educate future generations.Istanbul, Turkey is a city that effortlessly blends its rich historical past with its vibrant contemporary culture. One of the many aspects that make Istanbul truly special is its dynamic live music scene. For both locals and tourists, the city offers a multitude of live music venues that cater to diverse musical tastes, spanning genres from traditional Turkish music to jazz, rock, and electronic.

The heart of Istanbul's live music scene can often be found in the bustling neighborhood of Beyoglu, and specifically on Istiklal Avenue. Here, the streets are lined with an array of music clubs, bars, and concert halls that regularly host live performances. One of the most famous venues is the Babylon Bomonti, a premier destination for live music. Known for its eclectic programming, Babylon Bomonti features a variety of international and local artists, ranging from indie bands to world-renowned DJs.

Another iconic spot in Istanbul is Nardis Jazz Club, located in the historic Galata district. This intimate venue is a haven for jazz enthusiasts and has built a reputation for showcasing both up-and-coming and established jazz musicians. The club's cozy atmosphere and top-notch acoustics make it the ideal place to experience live jazz in Istanbul.

For those interested in traditional Turkish music, Kucukciftlik Park presents a unique blend of outdoor ambiance and cultural performances. This open-air venue hosts concerts that celebrate Turkey's rich musical heritage, often featuring traditional instruments such as the oud and ney. It is an excellent spot to immerse oneself in the sounds that have shaped Turkish music over the centuries.

In contrast, for those who lean towards more contemporary and electronic scenes, Zorlu Performing Arts Center is a modern venue that stages an array of performances, including some of the biggest names in the electronic music world. Located in the bustling neighborhood of Levent, this state-of-the-art facility attracts a younger crowd and provides a sleek, high-energy environment perfect for dance music events.

Lastly, for a more eclectic mix and a more intimate setting, Arkaoda in the Kadikoy district is a great choice. This bar and venue double as a community hub for local artists and musicians. It offers an ever-changing lineup and a relaxed atmosphere, making it a favorite among Istanbul's creative crowd.

In conclusion, Istanbul, Turkey, is a city where the live music scene thrives in various neighborhoods, offering something for everyone. Whether you are a fan of jazz, rock, electronic music, or traditional Turkish sounds, Istanbul's live music venues are vibrant spaces that bring people together to celebrate the universal love of music.Istanbul, Turkey, is a city that seamlessly blends the charm of its rich historical heritage with the vibrancy of modern life. Among its many attractions, the nightlife in Istanbul stands out as a testament to this remarkable fusion. The city boasts a diverse array of nightclubs and bars that cater to an assortment of tastes and preferences, making it a dynamic playground for locals and tourists alike.

As the sun sets over the Bosphorus, Istanbul's nightlife springs to life, offering a myriad of options for entertainment. One of the iconic areas for experiencing the city's nightlife is Beyoglu, particularly the district of Taksim. Here, the eclectic mix of venues ranges from traditional Turkish meyhanes to chic, contemporary bars. Istiklal Avenue in Taksim is often thronged with revelers moving from one venue to another, sampling what each has to offer. The street's cosmopolitan atmosphere is enhanced by the rhythmic beats of music spilling out from the assorted nightclubs and bars lining its expanse.

Galata, another prominent area, exudes a more artistic vibe. Many of its rooftop bars provide stunning views of the Golden Horn and the historic peninsula, offering a more relaxed yet equally enticing nightlife experience. The scenic backdrops, combined with expertly crafted cocktails, make for an unforgettable evening under the stars.

For those seeking luxury, the nightlife scene along the Bosphorus is unparalleled. High-end venues such as Reina and Sortie attract an elite crowd with their plush settings, exclusive events, and panoramic views of Istanbul's iconic skyline. These establishments often host international DJs and performers, ensuring that the entertainment is as elevated as the ambiance.

In contrast, Kadikoy on the Asian side of the city offers a more laid-back, bohemian experience. The district is filled with quirky bars and live music venues that offer a more intimate atmosphere. The area around Kadife Street, fondly nicknamed "Barlar Sokagi" or Bar Street, is particularly famous for its vibrant bar scene, attracting a younger, artistic crowd.

The diversity of Istanbul's nightlife is further exemplified by the multitude of genres of music available. From traditional Turkish live music and jazz to electronic dance music and rock, each venue offers its own unique flavor. Whether one wishes to dance the night away or simply relax with a drink in hand, the options are seemingly limitless.

In conclusion, Istanbul, Turkey, offers a nightlife experience that is as diverse and dynamic as the city itself. The array of nightclubs and bars cater to an extensive range of tastes, ensuring that every visitor can find their ideal evening entertainment. The vibrant energy, combined with breathtaking views and a rich cultural tapestry, makes Istanbul's nightlife an essential part of any visit to this captivating city.Istanbul, Turkey, is a city that not only straddles two continents but also boasts a rich tradition of theater and performing arts. Rooted in a history that spans millennia, Istanbul has evolved into a vibrant cultural hub where East meets West, creating a unique and diverse tapestry of artistic expression.

The theatrical scene in Istanbul can trace its origins back to ancient times. The city, formerly known as Byzantium and later Constantinople, was influenced by the Greeks and the Romans, who introduced various forms of theater. The remnants of ancient amphitheaters can still be found today, standing as testaments to the city's long-standing appreciation for the performing arts.

During the Ottoman Empire, Istanbul became a melting pot of cultures, which significantly influenced its theatrical traditions. The arts flourished under the patronage of the sultans, leading to the development of unique forms of drama, including shadow puppetry known as Karagoz and Hacivat. These traditional performances, often infused with humor and satire, have continued to be cherished and performed to this day.

In the modern era, Istanbul has grown to become a vibrant center for contemporary theater and performing arts. The city is home to numerous theaters, including the Istanbul State Theatre, which presents an eclectic mix of plays, from classical works to modern productions. The Istanbul Metropolitan Municipality City Theatres also play a significant role, offering a wide array of performances that cater to diverse audiences.

Furthermore, Istanbul hosts several international and national theater festivals that draw performers and spectators from around the globe. The Istanbul International Theatre Festival, held biennially, is a prestigious event that showcases avant-garde, experimental, and traditional performances. This festival not only highlights the talents of Turkish artists but also invites international performers, fostering a global exchange of artistic ideas.

In addition to traditional theater, Istanbul's performing arts scene encompasses a variety of genres, including dance, opera, and music. The Istanbul Opera House and the Ataturk Cultural Center are prominent venues that stage remarkable opera and ballet performances, blending classical and contemporary styles. The city's music scene is equally dynamic, ranging from Turkish classical music and folk dances to modern genres, thereby enriching its cultural landscape.

The influence of Istanbul's theater and performing arts extends beyond entertainment; it reflects the city's social and political milieu. Many contemporary Turkish playwrights and performers use the stage as a platform to address pressing societal issues, generating discourse and encouraging change. This aspect of the arts underscores the role of theater as a mirror to society, capturing the complexities and nuances of life in Istanbul.

In conclusion, Istanbul, Turkey, stands as a beacon of theater and performing arts, where historical traditions and modern innovations coexist harmoniously. The city's rich cultural heritage, combined with its ongoing artistic endeavors, ensures that Istanbul will continue to be a vital and inspiring destination for anyone interested in the performing arts.Major Annual Events in Istanbul, Turkey

Istanbul, Turkey, a city that straddles both Europe and Asia, thrives as a cultural and historical beacon. One of the characteristics that make this metropolitan area so vibrant is its array of major annual events that draw visitors from across the globe. Each year, Istanbul plays host to a plethora of festivals, trade fairs, and cultural events, offering something for everyone.

One of the most prominent events in Istanbul is the Istanbul Film Festival, which takes place every April. Founded in 1982, the festival has grown to become an internationally acknowledged event, screening renowned films, hosting esteemed directors, and providing a platform for filmmakerr across all genres. The festival not only highlights Turkish cinema but also garners a diverse collection of films from myriad countries, reflecting the city's role as a cultural crossroads.

In June, the city comes alive with the Istanbul Music Festival, organized by the Istanbul Foundation for Culture and Arts. This event, stretching through the summer months, offers a rich array of classical music performances. Renowned orchestras, individual virtuosos, and enthusiastic choirs fill the city's historic venues with melodious harmonies. These performances make the festival a much-anticipated event in the global classical music calendar.

In autumn, Istanbul welcomes the Istanbul Biennial, a contemporary art exhibition running from September to November, held every two years. Created by the Istanbul Foundation for Culture and Arts in 1987, the Biennial is internationally acclaimed, offering a stage for groundbreaking contemporary artworks and thought-provoking visual dialogues. It transforms the city into a giant public art gallery, drawing in art enthusiasts and critics alike.

Another notable event occurs in November, when Istanbul feeds the minds of literature enthusiasts with the Istanbul International Book Fair. This week-long event attracts authors, publishers, and readers from around the globe. It offers a rich tapestry of literary works, panel discussions, and book signings, celebrating the written word in numerous languages.

January is the month for food lovers, hosting the Istanbul Gastronomy Festival. This event showcases the richness of Turkish cuisine alongside international culinary traditions, featuring cooking competitions, workshops, and tastings. Chefs from around the world flock to Istanbul to participate, making it a foodie's paradise.

Alongside these major events, Istanbul also hosts the Istanbul Marathon every November, the Antique Book Fair, various jazz and rock festivals, and numerous cultural street fairs, ensuring that the city remains a dynamic and engaging place to visit throughout the entire year.

Overall, Istanbul's calendar of major annual events highlights the city's diversity and commitment to fostering a rich cultural milieu. Each event not only entertains and educates but also builds a sense of community, inviting people from around the world to discover and celebrate Istanbul's unique charm.Istanbul, Turkey is a city renowned for its cultural diversity, rich history, and breathtaking landscape. One of the most vivid ways in which Istanbul celebrates its heritage is through its seasonal festivals. These festivals, deeply ingrained in the fabric of the city, breathe life into its streets and offer a glimpse into the heart and soul of its people.

Spring in Istanbul is heralded by the International Istanbul Tulip Festival, a spectacle that sees millions of tulips in vibrant hues bloom across the city. The festival harks back to the Ottoman era when the tulip was a symbol of wealth and sophistication. Parks and public gardens, most notably Emirgan Park, become a canvas painted with colorful tulips, attracting locals and tourists alike to stroll through the magnificent displays. Music, art exhibitions, and various events complement the floral beauty, making the festival an immersive cultural experience.

Summer ushers in the Istanbul Music Festival, a celebration dedicated to classical music, opera, and ballet. This festival, organized by the Istanbul Foundation for Culture and Arts, attracts world-class musicians and performers to the city. Concerts are held in historical venues such as the Hagia Irene Museum, which adds a unique charm to the musical experience. The festival not only showcases established artists but also serves as a platform for emerging talents, fostering a vibrant music scene in the city.

Autumn in Istanbul is marked by the Istanbul Biennial, a contemporary art exhibition that transforms the city into an open-air museum. Artists from all over the globe converge in Istanbul to display their works in various venues, ranging from traditional galleries to public spaces. The Biennial challenges conventional art forms and encourages dialogue about social, political, and cultural issues. It is a period of intellectual engagement and creative expression, drawing art enthusiasts and critics from far and wide.

Winter in Istanbul is illuminated by the New Year's Eve celebrations, a time of collective revelry and reflection. The city streets, especially around Taksim Square and Istiklal Avenue, are adorned with festive lights and decorations. People from diverse backgrounds come together to bid farewell to the old year and welcome the new one with concerts, fireworks, and parties. The historic peninsula, with its stunning skyline of minarets and domes, provides a picturesque backdrop to the festivities, creating a magical atmosphere.

Istanbul's seasonal festivals are more than just events; they are a testament to the city's enduring spirit and its ability to blend tradition with modernity. Each season brings its own unique festival, enriching the lives of those who partake in them and knitting the community closer together. For anyone seeking to experience the true essence of Istanbul, joining in these celebrations is an unforgettable journey through the city's vibrant cultural tapestry.

Chapter 8: Bazaars of Istanbul Shopping Experience

Istanbul, Turkey is a vibrant city that seamlessly blends the old with the new, a characteristic that is especially evident in its diverse shopping areas. The main shopping areas in Istanbul are as much a testament to this cultural fusion as the city's renowned historical sites and modern infrastructure.

One of the most famous shopping destinations in Istanbul is the Grand Bazaar, or Kapali Carsi. Founded in the 15th century, the Grand Bazaar is one of the largest and oldest covered markets in the world. It boasts over 4,000 shops sprawled across a labyrinthine network of streets, offering a staggering array of goods from traditional Turkish carpets and ceramics to jewelry and spices. The bazaar is not just a place to shop, but a cultural experience that allows visitors to step back in time and feel the bustling ambiance of centuries past.

Another iconic shopping locale is Istiklal Street, an elegant pedestrian avenue lined with a mixture of high-end boutiques, art galleries, cafes, and bookstores. Stretching from Taksim Square to the historical Galata Tower, Istiklal Street is always alive with activity. Whether by day or night, visitors can explore a plethora of shops offering contemporary fashion, local brands, and internationally recognized names.

For modern retail therapy, Istanbul's shopping malls are second to none. The Zorlu Center, situated in the heart of the city, is a luxury shopping complex that combines high-end international brands with Turkish favorites. It also houses a variety of upscale restaurants and even a performing arts center, making it a destination for more than just shopping. Similarly, the Istanbul Cevahir Mall, one of the largest shopping malls in Europe, offers a wide range of shops, entertainment options, and dining facilities, catering to every need under one roof.

The Spice Bazaar, also known as Misir Carsisi, offers a more specialized shopping experience. Located in the Eminonu district, this vibrant bazaar is a sensory delight with its intoxicating mix of fragrances and colors. It is famous for its wide selection of spices, teas, dried fruits, nuts, and sweets like the iconic Turkish delight. Visiting the Spice Bazaar is a journey through the flavors and scents that define Turkish cuisine.

Istinye Park, another notable shopping center, combines indoor and outdoor shopping experiences with a unique architectural design. It houses a mix of luxury brands and popular retailers, along with an array of dining options from casual eateries to fine dining establishments. The mall also features a beautiful green area and an elegant glass dome, providing a pleasant shopping atmosphere.

Lastly, for those who enjoy a bohemian vibe, the Kadikoy Market on the Asian side of Istanbul offers an eclectic mix of boutiques, antique shops, and local designers. This area provides a more relaxed and alternative shopping experience compared to the bustling European side, reflecting the diverse and multifaceted nature of Istanbul.

In summary, Istanbul's main shopping areas offer a rich tapestry of experiences, from the traditional and historical to the modern and luxurious. Each area embodies a unique aspect of the city's character, making Istanbul not just a shopper's paradise, but also a cultural journey through its diverse heritage and contemporary life.Istanbul, Turkey is a city that exudes history, culture, and uniquely diverse street life. Among its numerous attractions, the specialty streets stand out as compelling destinations that encapsulate the essence of this vibrant metropolis. Each specialty street in Istanbul offers a distinct atmosphere, filled with aromas, sights, and sounds that cater to various interests, from shopping and dining to arts and crafts.

One of the most famous specialty streets is Istiklal Avenue, a bustling pedestrian thoroughfare in the heart of the city. Lined with an array of shops, cafes, art galleries, and historic buildings, Istiklal Avenue is a magnet for both locals and tourists. The scent of freshly roasted coffee mingles with the melodies of street musicians, creating an invigorating ambiance. Another highlight of this street is the historic tram that glides along its length, offering a nostalgic touch to the modern hustle and bustle.

Nearby, the Grand Bazaar, though technically a covered market, is essentially a labyrinth of specialty streets. Each lane within the Grand Bazaar is dedicated to different categories of goods, from intricate carpets and textiles to shimmering jewelry and gold. This marketplace acts as a sensory overload, with its vibrant colors, rich textures, and the sounds of merchants calling out their wares. It is a must-visit for anyone looking to experience the traditional commercial heart of Istanbul.

The vibrant Karakoy district offers another example of Istanbul's specialty streets. Known for its art galleries, contemporary cafes, and boutique shops, Karakoy has transformed from an industrial zone to a hip and trendy neighborhood. The street art that adorns many of its walls adds a splash of color and creativity, reflecting the dynamic energy of the local community. This area is particularly popular among young people and artists, who thrive in its eclectic environment.

For culinary enthusiasts, Kadikoy Market on the Asian side of Istanbul is an essential stop. This street is lined with a variety of food stalls and shops offering everything from fresh produce and spices to traditional Turkish delicacies like baklava and Turkish delight. The market gives insight into the city's rich culinary traditions and provides a feast for both the eyes and the palate.

Another unique specialty street is the antique district of Cukurcuma. Here, alleyways and small streets are filled with antique stores and vintage shops. From Ottoman relics to mid-century modern furniture, Cukurcuma attracts collectors and history buffs alike. The area's old-world charm and sense of nostalgia make it a delightful place to wander and explore.

In summary, the specialty streets of Istanbul, Turkey, offer a fascinating microcosm of the city's diverse and dynamic character. Whether you are exploring the commercial vibrancy of Istiklal Avenue, the historical richness of the Grand Bazaar, the artistic flair of Karakoy, the culinary delights of Kadikoy Market, or the antique treasures of Cukurcuma, each street provides a unique experience that contributes to the overall magic of Istanbul. These streets not only offer a glimpse into the city's past and present but also create lasting memories for those who walk along their paths.Istanbul, Turkey is a city that offers a rich blend of history, culture, and modernity. One of its most vibrant and captivating aspects is its bustling markets. Introductions to Istanbul are incomplete without experiencing its markets, which provide a window into the local life, traditions, and ingenuity of its people. Sprawling across various districts, each market in Istanbul has its unique charm and specialties.

The Grand Bazaar, known as Kapalıçarşı in Turkish, stands out as one of the largest and oldest covered markets in the world. Established in the 15th century, this maze of over 4,000 shops offers everything from intricately woven carpets to shimmering jewelry, ceramics, leather goods, and spices. Wandering through its alleys, visitors are often transported back in time, enchanted by the rich tapestry of colors, textures, and scents.

Another must-visit is the Spice Bazaar, or Mısır Çarşısı, which dates back to the 17th century. Located in the Eminönü district, this market is an aromatic paradise with stalls brimming with spices, dried fruits, nuts, and sweets. The air is filled with the heady blend of saffron, cloves, cinnamon, and an array of exotic spices that tickle the senses and evoke a bygone era of trade and adventure.

For a more contemporary market experience, the Kadıköy Market on the Asian side of the city presents an excellent option. This market is vibrant and lively, offering a mix of fresh produce, cheese, olives, and fish alongside trendy boutiques, cafes, and restaurants. It is a favorite among locals and provides a more modern take on the traditional market scene.

Additionally, Istanbul is home to several weekly markets, such as the Fatih Market, held on Wednesdays, and the Beşiktaş Market, held on Saturdays. These markets are a testament to the city's thriving community spirit, where vendors and shoppers engage in animated haggling and friendly banter, reflecting the warmth and hospitality that Istanbul is known for.

In conclusion, the markets of Istanbul, Turkey are much more than just places of commerce; they are dynamic landmarks where the past and present coalesce. Each market embodies a piece of Istanbul's soul, offering visitors not only the opportunity to purchase unique items but also to connect deeply with the city's rich heritage and vibrant culture. A visit to these markets allows one to truly grasp the essence of Istanbul, making it an unforgettable destination.What to Buy in Istanbul, Turkey

Istanbul, straddling two continents with a harmonious blend of East and West, is a city that offers a dizzying array of shopping opportunities. From bustling bazaars to modern shopping centers, the metropolis entices visitors to indulge in a medley of vibrant and unique items. For those wondering what to buy while visiting Istanbul, there are several iconic goods that make for unforgettable keepsakes or thoughtful gifts.

One of the most popular destinations for shoppers in Istanbul is the Grand Bazaar. This sprawling market, one of the oldest and largest covered markets in the world, is a treasure trove of traditional Turkish goods. Among the myriad of offerings, intricately designed carpets and kilims stand out. These handwoven textiles, often passed down through generations, reflect the rich cultural heritage of Anatolia. Collectors and casual buyers alike are drawn to their vivid colors and detailed patterns.

Not far from the Grand Bazaar lies the Egyptian Spice Bazaar, another historic hub of commerce. Here, shoppers are enveloped in the fragrant aromas of exotic spices, teas, and herbs. Saffron, sumac, and Turkish red pepper are among the must-buy items, prized for their quality and versatility in cooking. Additionally, Turkish delight, or lokum, a sweet confection that comes in a variety of flavors and textures, makes for a delightful and authentic edible souvenir.

For a more contemporary shopping experience, Istanbul's modern malls and boutiques provide a contrast to the traditional bazaars. In areas like Nisantasi and Istiklal Avenue, visitors can find stylish clothing, accessories, and home decor from both local designers and international brands. Turkish fashion has been gaining international recognition, making clothing and accessories from Istanbul both trendy and unique.

No visit to Istanbul would be complete without exploring its famous ceramics and pottery. The town of Iznik, just outside Istanbul, has been renowned for its distinctive blue-and-white tiles and pottery since the Ottoman era. These beautifully crafted items, ranging from plates and bowls to intricate tilework, add a splash of Turkish artistry to any home.

Istanbul is also famous for its high-quality leather goods. From jackets and bags to shoes and belts, Turkish leather products are celebrated for their craftsmanship and durability. The city's leather districts, such as Kazlicesme, offer a plethora of options, often at more competitive prices compared to Western countries.

Jewelry lovers will find themselves in paradise amidst Istanbul's many jewelry shops. The city is a historical center for gold and silversmithing. Traditional Ottoman designs, characterized by their intricate detail and use of gemstones, are particularly popular. Whether it's an elaborate necklace or a simple pair of earrings, Turkish jewelry offers something for every taste and budget.

Finally, Istanbul is known for its unique selection of Turkish tea sets and coffee pots. These beautifully decorated items are not only functional but also serve as exquisite pieces of art. The ornate designs often feature motifs inspired by nature and Ottoman architecture, making them a charming addition to any kitchen or dining room.

In conclusion, Istanbul, Turkey, offers a wealth of shopping experiences that cater to a wide range of tastes and interests. From the historical allure of its bazaars to the modern elegance of its shopping districts, the city is a paradise for those seeking both traditional and contemporary treasures. Whether it's spices, textiles, fashion, ceramics, leather goods, jewelry, or tea sets, Istanbul provides countless opportunities to bring a piece of its rich culture and history home.Istanbul, Turkey is a city renowned for its rich history, stunning architecture, and vibrant culture. Among the many treasures it offers is an impressive array of local crafts that reflect the citys diverse heritage and the skilled artisans who call it home. These crafts tell a story of centuries-old traditions, passed down through generations, evolving yet retaining their original charm.

One of the most iconic local crafts of Istanbul is Turkish ceramics. Istanbul's ceramic art is particularly famous for its Iznik tiles, known for their bold blue-and-white designs, often adorned with intricate floral patterns and geometric motifs. The craftsmanship involved in creating these tiles is meticulous, requiring both artistic ability and a deep understanding of the materials and techniques. The legacy of Iznik ceramics is visible in many of the citys historic buildings, including the grand mosques and palaces where these tiles serve as stunning decorative elements.

Another jewel in the crown of Istanbul's local crafts is the art of carpet weaving. Turkish carpets, especially those originating from Istanbul, are celebrated worldwide for their quality, durability, and exquisite patterns. These carpets are often made from high-quality wool or silk and dyed using natural colors, preserving the traditional methods that date back hundreds of years. Each carpet tells a unique story through its design, where every knot is carefully tied by hand, making every piece a true work of art.

Leatherwork is also a notable craft in Istanbul. The citys artisans produce finely crafted leather goods, including shoes, bags, and belts, using time-honored techniques. The Grand Bazaar, one of the oldest and largest covered markets in the world, is a perfect place to explore this craft. Here, you can find an array of leather products that show the same attention to detail and quality that has made Turkish leatherwork renowned worldwide.

Jewelry making is another traditional craft that thrives in Istanbul. The city has long been a hub for goldsmiths and jewelers, whose workshops produce intricate pieces featuring precious metals and gemstones. The craftsmanship often incorporates both Ottoman and modern designs, creating unique pieces that are both timeless and contemporary. The jewelry district, located along the historic streets near the Grand Bazaar, is a testament to this enduring craft, where one can find everything from ornate necklaces to delicate rings.

Lastly, Turkish calligraphy and marbling, known as Ebru, showcase the artistic spirit of Istanbul. These arts involve a high degree of skill and creativity, transforming simple materials like paper and ink into beautiful works of art. Ebru, in particular, is a mesmerizing process where pigments are floated on water and then transferred to paper, creating one-of-a-kind patterns that resemble marble.

In conclusion, the local crafts of Istanbul offer a window into the soul of this ancient city. They represent not just the skill and creativity of its artisans, but also the cultural heritage that makes Istanbul a unique and fascinating place. From ceramics and carpets to leatherwork, jewelry, and calligraphy, the crafts of Istanbul continue to enchant both locals and visitors, preserving the legacy of one of the worlds most historically rich cities.Unique Finds in Istanbul, Turkey

Istanbul, Turkey's largest city and a mesmerizing blend of ancient traditions and modern vibrancy, offers a multitude of unique finds that captivate the soul of any wanderer. Straddling both Europe and Asia, this historic metropolis is a tapestry woven with threads of diverse cultures and centuries of history. Travelers to Istanbul often find themselves lost in its labyrinthine streets, stumbling upon hidden treasures that tell stories of a bygone era while embracing the pulse of contemporary life.

One of the most striking unique finds in Istanbul is its bustling bazaars. The Grand Bazaar, known locally as Kapali Carsi, is one of the oldest and largest covered markets in the world. It is a sensory overload of colors, sounds, and smells, where merchants beckon from stalls laden with exotic spices, intricate carpets, and glittering jewelry. Each corner turned within its winding alleys reveals another layer of history and craftsmanship that has been passed down through generations.

Not far from these lively markets lies another gem, the Spice Bazaar. Officially named Misir Carsisi, this market specializes in an array of aromatic spices, dried fruits, and local delicacies. Walking through its vibrant stalls, visitors can discover a world of flavors bound in small, colorful piles, each with its own distinct fragrance and story. The alluring scents of saffron, sumac, and Turkish delight create an olfactory experience that is as compelling as it is unforgettable.

Away from the bustling markets, Istanbul's architectural marvels present unique finds that echo the grandeur of the past. The Hagia Sophia, with its majestic domes and awe-inspiring mosaics, stands as a testament to the city's rich Byzantine legacy. Originally built as a cathedral, it has served various roles as a mosque and museum over the centuries, each transformation adding to its profound historical narrative. Similarly, the Blue Mosque, or Sultan Ahmed Mosque, dazzles visitors with its six minarets and the stunning blue tiles that adorn its interior. Both structures offer a glimpse into the spiritual and architectural ingenuity that has shaped Istanbul's skyline.

For those seeking quieter moments of discovery, Istanbul's hidden courtyards and tea gardens offer serene retreats within the urban sprawl. Yerebatan Sarnici, also known as the Basilica Cistern, is an underground marvel that reveals the city's ancient ingenuity in water storage. It is a cavernous space supported by rows of columns, silently narrating tales from the depths of Byzantine engineering.

In the realm of culinary delights, Istanbul serves up unique finds that tantalize the taste buds. Street vendors and modest eateries offer a chance to savor traditional foods like simit, a sesame-encrusted bread, or balik ekmek, fish sandwiches freshly prepared along the Eminonu waterfront. Each bite captures the essence of the city's diverse culinary heritage, blending influences from across the Ottoman Empire era and beyond.

As the city continues to evolve, modern finds also make their mark on Istanbul's eclectic landscape. Trendy neighborhoods like Karakoy and Beyoglu are home to contemporary art galleries, chic boutiques, and innovative eateries that showcase Istanbul's dynamic present. Here, street art and cutting-edge design coexist with remnants of the past, crafting a unique atmosphere that reflects the city's endless capacity for reinvention.

In conclusion, Istanbul, Turkey, is a treasure trove of unique finds that span the spectrum of human history and creativity. From its ancient bazaars and monumental architecture to its hidden corners and modern marvels, Istanbul invites exploration and leaves an indelible imprint on all who visit. Each discovery within this enigmatic city reveals a piece of its soul, inviting travelers to delve deeper into its enduring magic.

Chapter 9: Istanbul's Adventure Playground

Istanbul, Turkey is a city where the East meets the West, rich in history and culture. Yet, amidst its bustling streets and historical landmarks, the city boasts an impressive selection of parks where locals and visitors can find tranquility and a connection with nature. These green spaces serve as urban oases, offering a respite from the vibrant city life.

One of the most famous parks in Istanbul is Gulhane Park, which translates to "House of Roses." This park holds a significant place in Turkish history, as it once belonged to the outer garden of Topkapi Palace. Today, Gulhane Park is open to all, offering beautifully landscaped gardens, walking paths, and a variety of trees and flowers that change with the seasons. It is an ideal spot for a leisurely stroll or a quiet moment of reflection.

Another notable green space is Yildiz Park. This expansive park in the Besiktas district is known for its diverse flora and scenic views. Formerly a part of the Yildiz Palace complex, the park encompasses serene lakes, charming pavilions, and well-maintained gardens. With its rolling hills and shaded paths, Yildiz Park is a favorite among joggers and nature enthusiasts.

Emirgan Park is also one of Istanbul's finest. Nestled along the Bosphorus in the Sariyer district, it is particularly famous for its annual Tulip Festival in April, where millions of tulips bloom in various colors and patterns. The park also features three historical pavilions that now serve as restaurants and cafes, offering visitors a unique dining experience amidst lush greenery.

For those who seek modern recreational areas, Macka Park provides a contemporary urban escape. Situated close to the luxury district of Nisantasi, it features jogging tracks, outdoor exercise equipment, and playgrounds for children. The park's design caters to both tranquil walks and active lifestyles, making it a versatile spot for different age groups.

Finally, Fenerbahce Park is a charming waterfront park located in the Kadikoy district on the Asian side of Istanbul. Overlooking the Marmara Sea, the park is filled with walking paths, picnic areas, and an array of cafes that offer stunning sea views. It is a perfect place for a family outing or a romantic evening by the water.

These parks are just a few examples of the many green spaces Istanbul offers. Each park provides a unique experience, from historical ambiance and cultural festivities to modern amenities and natural beauty. Together, they contribute to the city's charm, making Istanbul not only a place of historical and architectural significance but also a city that nurtures its natural landscapes for all to enjoy.Istanbul, Turkey, is a city renowned for its rich historical tapestry, vibrant culture, and dynamic urban landscape. Amidst this bustling metropolis lies a serene sanctuary known as the city's botanical gardens. These green spaces offer a tranquil escape from the city's energetic pace and provide visitors with an opportunity to immerse themselves in nature's splendor.

The botanical gardens in Istanbul are meticulously maintained and showcase an impressive collection of flora from around the world. As visitors meander through the winding paths, they encounter an array of plant species, each meticulously labeled with botanical names and informative descriptions. These gardens are not only a feast for the eyes but also serve as an educational haven for those interested in botany and horticulture.

One of the most captivating aspects of Istanbul's botanical gardens is their seasonal diversity. In spring, the gardens come alive with a kaleidoscope of blooming flowers, their vibrant colors and fragrances filling the air. Summer brings lush greenery and the pleasant shade of ancient trees, providing a cool retreat from the city's heat. Autumn transforms the gardens into a canvas of warm hues as leaves turn golden and crimson. Even in winter, the gardens hold a unique charm, with evergreen plants standing resilient amid the colder temperatures.

The botanical gardens are not merely a collection of plants but a hub of biodiversity and conservation efforts. Many of the gardens collaborate with research institutions and participate in programs aimed at preserving endangered plant species. This commitment to conservation ensures that future generations will continue to enjoy the same botanical wonders that captivate visitors today.

Moreover, the gardens play host to a variety of cultural events and festivals throughout the year. From guided tours and educational workshops to musical performances and art exhibitions, these events add a vibrant cultural dimension to the natural beauty of the gardens. They bring together locals and tourists alike, fostering a sense of community and shared appreciation for the environment.

For those looking to unwind, the botanical gardens offer numerous tranquil spots ideal for relaxation and reflection. Benches scattered throughout the gardens invite visitors to sit and soak in the serene ambiance. Small ponds and water features create soothing sounds that enhance the overall sense of peace and tranquility.

In conclusion, the botanical gardens in Istanbul, Turkey, are a hidden gem that exemplifies the city's unique blend of natural beauty and cultural richness. Whether you are a nature enthusiast, a scholar of plant sciences, or simply someone seeking a moment of calm amid the urban hustle, these gardens offer an unforgettable experience. The harmonious coexistence of diverse plant life and vibrant cultural activities within the gardens underscores Istanbul's remarkable ability to marry tradition and modernity, nature and city life.Popular Trails where the City Name is Istanbul, Turkey.

Istanbul, a city that straddles two continents, offers an array of stunning and historic trails that cater to both the casual stroller and the avid hiker. Istanbul's unique geographical position on the banks of the Bosphorus, combined with its rich historical and cultural legacy, makes it a prime location for exploring on foot. From scenic coastal walks to rugged forest paths, the city has something to offer everyone.

One of the most popular trails in Istanbul is the Bosphorus Walk. This iconic route spans both the European and Asian sides of the city, offering unparalleled views of the Bosphorus Strait. Starting from the lively neighborhood of Ortakoy, the trail meanders past historic palaces, mosques, and vibrant marketplaces, eventually leading to the serene and prestigious district of Arnavutkoy. Along the way, walkers can enjoy the refreshing sea breeze and the sight of numerous ships navigating the waters. The mixture of modern urban life with historical architecture makes this a must-see trail.

For those seeking a more immersive natural experience, the Belgrad Forest provides a verdant escape from the hustle and bustle of city life. Located on the northern edge of Istanbul, this expansive forest offers several well-maintained trails, ranging from short loops to more challenging hikes. The 6.5-kilometer-long Büyükdere Trail is particularly popular, winding through lush forests, past serene lakes, and even traces of ancient aqueducts. It is a haven for nature lovers, with opportunities for bird watching and spotting various flora and fauna that thrive in this protected area.

The Princes' Islands also offer a unique trail experience just a short ferry ride away from the mainland. The islands are car-free, ensuring a peaceful walking environment. The largest of these islands, Büyükada, features trails that take visitors along the coastline, through quaint villages, and up to the island's highest peak, Aya Yorgi Hill. Hikers are rewarded with panoramic views of the Sea of Marmara and the Istanbul skyline in the distance. The islands also boast lush landscapes and historic buildings that provide a glimpse into the past.

Another noteworthy trail is the path that leads to Camlica Hill, one of the highest points in Istanbul. Situated on the Asian side of the city, this trail offers sweeping views of the entire cityscape, the Bosphorus, and beyond. Starting from the bustling district of Uskudar, the trail ascends through residential neighborhoods and verdant parks, eventually leading to a picturesque summit adorned with tea gardens and picnic areas. It is an ideal spot to witness a sunrise or sunset over the city.

In essence, Istanbul's popular trails offer a diverse array of experiences that capture the essence of the city's unique blend of history, culture, and natural beauty. Whether strolling along the vibrant shoreline of the Bosphorus, hiking through the tranquil Belgrad Forest, exploring the car-free paths of the Princes' Islands, or ascending the heights of Camlica Hill, visitors are sure to find a trail that resonates with their sense of adventure and exploration. Istanbul, with its multifaceted charm, continues to be a premier destination for walkers and hikers from around the world.Istanbul, Turkey, is a city where the stunning collision of continents creates an unparalleled experience for travelers and residents alike. Woven through its intricate tapestry of history, culture, and architecture are various scenic routes that offer glimpses into the heart of this vibrant metropolis. One of the most iconic routes is along the Bosphorus Strait, where the city's striking juxtaposition of Asia and Europe becomes vividly clear. A leisurely ferry ride along this waterway reveals a panorama of majestic palaces, quaint fishing villages, and grandiose mansions that line the shores. The Bosphorus Bridge, an engineering marvel connecting the two continents, stands as a testament to Istanbul's unique geographical and cultural significance.

Venturing into the historic peninsula, another scenic path unfolds through the ancient district of Sultanahmet. Here, every step is a walk through time. The breathtaking views of the Blue Mosque, with its imposing domes and minarets, are complemented by the adjacent Hagia Sophia, a structure that has stood as both a church and a mosque over the centuries. Nearby, the vistas from the gardens of Topkapi Palace provide a serene counterpoint, offering a picturesque overlook of the Golden Horn and the sprawling city beyond.

For those who prefer the verdant beauty of parks and gardens, a stroll through Gulhane Park is a perfect choice. Once the royal garden of the Ottoman sultans, this lush expanse offers tranquil pathways that meander past colorful flowerbeds, shady groves, and the historic Column of the Goths. The park's elevated points provide sweeping views of the Bosphorus, particularly enchanting during the late afternoon when the fading sunlight casts a golden glow over the water.

Another notable scenic route is the Istiklal Avenue in the district of Beyoglu. This bustling pedestrian street is vibrant with energy and alive with the sounds of street musicians, inviting cafes, and historic trams that clatter along its length. As one walks towards Taksim Square, the heart of modern Istanbul, the mix of neoclassical and contemporary architecture evokes the dynamic fusion that defines the city.

Lastly, a journey up to Camlica Hill offers one of the most expansive views of Istanbul. From this elevated vantage point on the Asian side, sweeping vistas encompass the Bosphorus, the Sea of Marmara, and the skyline peppered with minarets and skyscrapers. The hilltop gardens here provide a peaceful retreat, allowing visitors to soak in the city's beauty from above.

In Istanbul, scenic routes are more than just pathways; they are avenues to understanding the deep historical layers and vibrant contemporary life of this illustrious city. Whether by land or sea, each route invites travelers to explore and savor the distinct blend of tradition and modernity that makes Istanbul truly unique.Best Beaches in Istanbul, Turkey

Istanbul, Turkey, a city that straddles two continents, is renowned for its rich history, stunning architecture, and vibrant culture. One aspect of Istanbul that often remains underappreciated is its beautiful beaches. Nestled between the sparkling waters of the Bosphorus, the Sea of Marmara, and the Black Sea, Istanbul offers a variety of scenic seaside retreats that provide a refreshing escape from the bustling city life.

A notable beach that stands out is Florya Beach, located on the European side, not far from the Ataturk International Airport. This beach is easily accessible and features a long stretch of sand perfect for sunbathing. The calm waters of the Sea of Marmara make it an ideal place for swimming. Furthermore, Florya Beach Park offers shaded areas, cafes, and restaurants, allowing visitors to enjoy a leisurely day by the sea while also satisfying their culinary cravings.

On the Asian side of Istanbul lies Caddebostan Beach, a popular destination for both locals and tourists. This beach is part of a series of small, pleasant beaches and parks along the Marmara shoreline. It is well-maintained and equipped with changing cabins, sun loungers, and umbrellas. The nearby Bağdat Avenue, renowned for its vibrant shopping and dining options, adds to the beach's appeal, making it a perfect spot for combining a beach day with some urban exploration.

Kilyos Beach, also known as Kylios Beach, located on the Black Sea coast, is another outstanding choice for beach lovers. Situated about 30 kilometers from the city center, Kilyos offers a more rustic and natural beach experience. The long sandy beach backed by dunes and greenery is perfect for a tranquil retreat. Kilyos is particularly popular among surfers and windsurfers, thanks to its strong winds and waves. Several beach clubs and cafes can be found in the area, providing amenities and entertainment.

For those seeking a more exclusive experience, Sile Beach is a must-visit. Located further northeast on the Black Sea coast, Sile is known for its stunning cliffs, golden sand, and crystal-clear waters. This beach offers a picturesque setting for both relaxation and adventure. Nearby, the charming Sile village with its historic lighthouse and castle adds a touch of cultural allure to the beach outing.

Finally, Buyukada Beach, situated on the largest of the Princes Islands, provides a unique and serene beach experience. The island is accessible by a short ferry ride from Istanbul and is known for its prohibition of motor vehicles, which ensures a peaceful atmosphere.

The beach itself offers beautiful views, clean waters, and a laid-back vibe. Visitors can also explore the island by bicycle or horse-drawn carriage and enjoy the local seafood delicacies.

In conclusion, Istanbul's beaches offer a diverse range of experiences for those looking to unwind by the sea. Whether it is the urban convenience of Florya and Caddebostan beaches, the natural charm of Kilyos and Sile, or the tranquil beauty of Buyukada, Istanbul has a beach destination to suit every taste. These coastal gems add yet another dimension to the city's rich tapestry, making Istanbul a truly multifaceted travel destination.Istanbul, Turkey is a city of contrasts, weaving together a rich tapestry of ancient history and modern vibrancy, all framed by the sparkling waters that surround it. Nestled between the Bosphorus Strait, the Sea of Marmara, and the Golden Horn, Istanbul offers an array of water activities that tap into the heart of its unique geographical splendor.

One of the most iconic water activities in Istanbul is taking a cruise along the Bosphorus. These cruises allow visitors to see the city's most famous landmarks from a serene perspective on the water. From opulent Ottoman palaces like Dolmabahce and Beylerbeyi to the imposing medieval fortresses of Rumeli Hisari and Anadolu Hisari, a Bosphorus cruise provides an unparalleled view of Istanbul's historical architecture. These leisurely voyages often include guided tours that delve into the fascinating stories behind these structures, making the experience both relaxing and educational.

For those seeking a more hands-on adventure, there are several options for kayaking in Istanbul's waterways. Paddling along the Bosphorus or the Sea of Marmara offers a refreshing way to experience the city. Kayakers can explore hidden coves, waterfront neighborhoods, and even paddle close to historic sites, such as the Maiden's Tower, which stands proudly on a small islet in the Bosphorus. Kayaking allows a unique, close-to-nature approach to experiencing Istanbul's aquatic scenery.

Fishing enthusiasts can indulge in their hobby along the city's abundant shores. The Galata Bridge, which spans the Golden Horn, is particularly famous for its fishing. Here, both locals and tourists can be seen casting their lines, hoping to catch a variety of fish that inhabit these waters. Fishing in Istanbul is not only a peaceful pastime but also a cultural experience, as it provides an opportunity to mingle with locals and perhaps enjoy a traditional fish sandwich from one of the nearby vendors afterward.

For a more relaxed day on the water, visitors can head to the Princes' Islands, a group of nine islands in the Sea of Marmara. The islands are accessible by ferry from the city and offer numerous water activities such as swimming, sailing, and even stand-up paddleboarding. The tranquil atmosphere of the islands, free from motor traffic, provides a stark contrast to the bustling city atmosphere, allowing visitors to unwind and take in the natural beauty.

In Istanbul, the interplay of land and water creates a vibrant setting for a variety of aquatic adventures. Whether it is a scenic cruise, an active kayak trip, a lazy day of fishing, or exploring the Princes' Islands, there is no shortage of ways to connect with the city's waters. Each activity offers a distinctive glimpse into the life and history of Istanbul, making water activities an essential part of the Istanbul experience.

Chapter 10: Istanbul Adventures: Day Trips & Excursions

Istanbul, Turkey, is a city that bridges two continents, Europe and Asia, and offers a blend of history, culture, and modernity. Beyond the bustling streets and historic landmarks of Istanbul's urban core lie surrounding areas that are equally captivating and offer their own unique highlights.

First, the Princes' Islands are a group of nine islands in the Sea of Marmara, just a short ferry ride from Istanbul. These islands provide an escape from the city's hustle and bustle. Cars are banned, and transportation is mainly by bicycle or horse-drawn carriage, preserving their tranquil atmosphere. Büyükada, the largest of the islands, is known for its beautiful Ottoman-era mansions and lush pine forests.

To the north of Istanbul is the Belgrad Forest, a vast green space that serves as the lungs of the city. It is a popular spot for hiking, picnicking, and nature photography. The Atatürk Arboretum within the forest is a botanical garden featuring a diverse collection of plant species, ideal for anyone seeking a peaceful retreat into nature.

East of the city lies the Anatolian side, often less frequented by tourists but rich in attractions. The district of Kadıköy is renowned for its vibrant arts scene, bustling markets, and lively nightlife. It offers a more local experience compared to the more touristy European side. Üsküdar, another district on the Anatolian side, is home to historic mosques and the picturesque Maiden's Tower, also known as Leander's Tower, which is perched on a small islet at the entrance of the Bosphorus Strait.

For those interested in history, the town of Edirne, located to the west of Istanbul, is a treasure trove of Ottoman architecture. The Selimiye Mosque, a UNESCO World Heritage site, stands as a masterpiece of the famous architect Mimar Sinan. Edirne is also famous for its annual oil-wrestling festival, which is one of the oldest sporting events in the world.

To the south, the Marmara coast boasts beautiful beaches and seaside towns. The city of Yalova is known for its thermal hot springs and natural beauty. Just a short ferry ride away, it offers a perfect getaway for relaxation and leisure.

Additionally, the Thrace Wine Route, northwest of Istanbul, takes you through picturesque vineyards and wineries. Visitors can explore the rich winemaking tradition of the region, taste local wines, and enjoy the scenic countryside.

In conclusion, while Istanbul itself is a city brimming with life and historical wonders, its surrounding areas offer equally fascinating experiences. From serene islands and lush forests to historic towns and vibrant districts, each area enhances the allure of visiting Istanbul, making it a truly diverse and enriching destination.Istanbul, Turkey - Cultural and Historical Sites

Istanbul, Turkey is a city that is both ancient and modern, vibrantly living in the present while deeply rooted in its rich and diverse history. As the meeting point of Europe and Asia, this city offers a unique blend of cultures, traditions, and histories, all waiting to be explored by curious visitors. One of the most iconic historical sites in Istanbul is the Hagia Sophia, a magnificent structure that has served as a church, a mosque, and now a museum. Built in the 6th century during the reign of Emperor Justinian, the Hagia Sophia is renowned for its massive dome and stunning mosaics, exemplifying the architectural prowess of the Byzantine Empire.

Another must-visit site is the Topkapi Palace, which was the primary residence and administrative headquarters of the Ottoman sultans for nearly 400 years. The palace is a sprawling complex of courtyards, chambers, and gardens, each telling a story of the opulent lifestyles and vast influence of the Ottoman Empire. Visitors can marvel at the exquisite architecture, intricate tile work, and the extensive collection of artifacts, including the famous Topkapi Dagger and the Spoonmaker's Diamond.

The Blue Mosque, officially known as Sultan Ahmed Mosque, is another historical gem in Istanbul. Constructed in the early 17th century, it is an architectural masterpiece with its six minarets and a series of cascading domes. Inside, visitors are greeted by tens of thousands of blue Iznik tiles that give the mosque its popular name. The Blue Mosque continues to function as a place of worship, allowing visitors to experience the spiritual ambiance of an active Islamic site.

Istanbul is also home to the ancient Hippodrome, which was once the social heart of Constantinople, the capital of the Byzantine Empire. Although much of it lies in ruins today, the Hippodrome's surviving structures, such as the Serpent Column and the Obelisk of Theodosius, offer glimpses into its grand past where chariot races and public gatherings were held.

A visit to Istanbul would not be complete without exploring the vibrant Grand Bazaar, one of the oldest and largest covered markets in the world. With its labyrinthine alleys and countless stalls selling everything from spices and textiles to jewelry and ceramics, the Grand Bazaar is a sensory delight that captures the bustling commercial spirit of Istanbul through the ages.

Equally captivating is the Basilica Cistern, an underground marvel built in the 6th century to store water for the city. With its forest of ancient columns reflected in the shallow waters, the cistern provides a serene and mystical atmosphere unlike any other historical site.

These cultural and historical sites in Istanbul not only highlight the city's extraordinary past but also its continued significance as a bridge between continents and civilizations. Each site offers a unique window into the intricate tapestry of history that has shaped Istanbul into the dynamic and captivating city it is today. Whether you are drawn by the grandeur of its monuments or the charm of its bustling bazaars, Istanbul promises a journey through time that is both enriching and unforgettable.Istanbul, Turkey is a city that seamlessly blends ancient history with modernity, and its diverse natural landscapes are no exception to this harmonious mix. One of the unique features of Istanbul is its collection of national parks, offering both locals and visitors a chance to escape the bustling urban environment and immerse themselves in nature.

One of the most renowned parks in Istanbul is the Belgrad Forest. Located on the European side of the city, this sprawling forest is a haven for outdoor enthusiasts. Covering over 5,000 hectares, Belgrad Forest offers an extensive network of walking and cycling trails, making it an ideal spot for hiking, jogging, or simply enjoying a peaceful walk amidst lush greenery. The forest also contains several reservoirs and picnic areas, where families often gather for a day out in nature.

Another notable natural retreat is Parkorman, an urban park that combines recreational activities with natural beauty. Situated closer to the heart of the city, Parkorman provides a green oasis for those seeking a quick getaway without venturing too far from the urban center. The park features numerous walking paths, open spaces for sports, and playgrounds, making it a popular destination for families and fitness enthusiasts alike.

Polonezkoy Nature Park is another gem located on the Asian side of Istanbul. Originally established by Polish settlers in the 19th century, this village-turned-nature park is now a protected area celebrated for its rich biodiversity and cultural heritage. Visitors to Polonezkoy can explore its scenic walking trails, visit the small village museum, and experience the charming blend of Turkish and Polish influences that have shaped the area.

The Camlica Hill Nature Park offers breathtaking panoramic views of Istanbul. Divided into two sections, Big Camlica and Little Camlica, this park is a favorite among locals for both daytime picnics and evening outings. The park is adorned with beautiful gardens, fountains, and observation terraces, making it a perfect spot to watch the sunset over the city skyline.

Lastly, Aydos Hill and its surrounding parklands present another delightful escape. Aydos Hill is the highest point in Istanbul, offering a picturesque view of the city and the Marmara Sea. The area is well-suited for various outdoor activities, including hiking, horseback riding, and bird-watching, providing a diverse range of experiences for nature lovers.

In conclusion, Istanbul's national parks are an integral part of the city's charm, providing much-needed green spaces within its urban expanse. These parks not only preserve the natural beauty and biodiversity of the region but also offer recreational and cultural experiences that enrich the lives of both residents and tourists. Whether seeking adventure, relaxation, or simply a breath of fresh air, the national parks of Istanbul, Turkey, serve as treasured sanctuaries that highlight the city's commitment to harmonizing nature with urban life.Istanbul, Turkey is a city that seamlessly blends the old with the new, offering a multitude of scenic spots that captivate both residents and visitors alike. Straddling the continents of Europe and Asia, it is a place where ancient history and modern living coexist harmoniously. Among its many attractions, the Bosphorus Strait stands out as one of the most iconic natural landmarks. This narrow, natural waterway not only divides the city but also provides a breathtaking backdrop for a variety of activities, from leisurely boat cruises to scenic waterfront dining.

The historic Sultanahmet District is home to several of the city's most famous landmarks. Here, the mesmerizing Hagia Sophia, with its massive dome and stunning mosaics, stands as a testament to the architectural prowess of the Byzantine Empire. Nearby, the Blue Mosque dazzles with its six minarets and intricate blue tilework, offering a serene place for reflection and admiration. The Topkapi

Palace, a grand imperial residence, now serves as a museum displaying Ottoman treasures and rich historical artifacts.

For those seeking a panoramic view of this vibrant city, a visit to Galata Tower is essential. This medieval stone tower offers a 360-degree view of Istanbul and is especially popular at sunset, when the city is bathed in hues of orange and pink. Below, the bustling Istiklal Avenue stretches out, inviting visitors to explore its myriad of shops, cafes, and cultural venues.

Further exploration leads to the Grand Bazaar, one of the largest and oldest covered markets in the world. With over 4,000 shops, the bazaar is a labyrinth of colors, sounds, and scents, offering everything from handcrafted jewelry to aromatic spices. It is a true sensory overload that captures the essence of Istanbul's vibrant trade history.

As one ventures into the Asian side of the city, the neighborhood of Kadikoy offers a more laid-back atmosphere. With its lively market streets, cozy cafes, and stunning views of the Bosphorus, it is a charming area to explore and unwind.

In contrast, the opulent Dolmabahce Palace on the European side showcases the Western influence on Ottoman architecture. Built in the 19th century, its lavish interiors and meticulously manicured gardens provide a glimpse into the grandeur of the Ottoman era.

Nature lovers will find solace in the serene beauty of the Princes' Islands, a short ferry ride from the mainland. These car-free islands are perfect for cycling, horse-drawn carriage rides, or simply enjoying the pristine beaches and lush greenery.

In Istanbul, each scenic spot tells a story, weaving together the threads of different cultures, empires, and traditions. It is a city where every corner holds a piece of history, yet continually pulses with the energy of modern urban life, making it a truly unique and enchanting destination.Istanbul, Turkey is a city that stands as a bridge between two continents, Asia and Europe, and is richly embroidered with a tapestry of history spanning over millennia. Among its meandering streets and bustling bazaars lie some of the world's most remarkable historical locations, each narrating stories of empires, conquest, and cultural amalgamation.

One of the most iconic landmarks in Istanbul is the Hagia Sophia. Originally constructed in 537 AD during the reign of Byzantine Emperor Justinian I, it served as a cathedral for nearly a thousand years before being converted into a mosque in 1453 following the Ottoman conquest of the city. In 1935, it was turned into a museum by the Republic of Turkey, and most recently, it has been reconverted into a mosque. The Hagia Sophia is renowned for its stunning architectural marvels, including the massive dome that seemingly floats above, an engineering feat of its time.

Adjacent to the Hagia Sophia lies another monumental relic, the Blue Mosque, formally known as the Sultan Ahmed Mosque. Completed in 1616, under the orders of Sultan Ahmed I, the Blue Mosque astonishes visitors with its six minarets and a distinct cascade of domes. The interior is adorned with over 20,000 handmade ceramic tiles in varying shades of blue, illuminating the vast space with a serene glow.

A short walk from these grandeur edifices is the Topkapi Palace, an epicenter of the Ottoman Empire's power for nearly 400 years. Building commenced shortly after the conquest of Constantinople in 1453, and the palace served as the residence of Ottoman sultans, as well as the administrative and educational core of the empire. Within its expansive courtyards and opulent rooms, visitors can find treasures such as the Prophet Muhammad's cloak and sword, a poignant manifestation of the empire's extensive reach and deep-seated traditions.

The Basilica Cistern, also known as the Yerebatan Sarnici, is an ancient marvel hidden beneath the city's surface. Constructed in 532 AD by order of Emperor Justinian I, the cistern once supplied water to the Great Palace and surrounding buildings. With its forest of marble columns rising from the water, creating an ethereal atmosphere, it mirrors the intricate and hidden layers of Istanbul's historical depth.

Further exploring the rich historical heritage, there is the Grand Bazaar, one of the largest and oldest covered markets in the world. Established in 1461, it retains its place as a bustling hub of trade and commerce, featuring over 4,000 shops spread across 61 covered streets. It is a place where one can still feel the pulse of the ancient Silk Road, echoing the footsteps of traders and travelers who once passed through its grand arches.

Lastly, standing tall and offering panoramic vistas of the city is the Galata Tower. This medieval stone tower was built in 1348 during the reign of the Genoese colony in Constantinople. Over centuries, it has served various purposes, including as a watchtower and even a prison. Today, it offers one of the best viewpoints to observe the unique skyline of Istanbul, where ancient history and modern life blend seamlessly.

Each of these historical locations in Istanbul tells a portion of the city's extensive narrative, showcasing a blend of Byzantine, Roman, and Ottoman influences, and reinforcing its status as a city where East meets West. Istanbul's historical sites are not mere remnants of the past; they are living chronicles that continue to shape the cultural and social fabric of this remarkable metropolis.Tips for Visiting Istanbul, Turkey

Istanbul, Turkey, offers an exquisite blend of cultures, history, and vibrant urban life. Its unique position straddling two continents, Europe and Asia, gives it a distinct atmosphere that attracts travelers from around the world. To make the most of your visit to this captivating city, here are some essential tips to consider.

First and foremost, make sure to plan your visit during spring or autumn. These seasons provide the most pleasant weather, avoiding the scorching summer heat and the chill of winter. Istanbul can get crowded, especially during peak tourist seasons, so try to book accommodations and major attractions in advance to ensure availability and avoid long waiting times.

When packing for your trip, remember that Istanbul is a city of steep hills and cobblestone streets. Comfortable walking shoes are a must as you will likely spend a lot of time exploring on foot. Modest clothing is also recommended, especially if you plan to visit any of the numerous mosques, including the iconic Blue Mosque where appropriate attire is required.

Navigating the city can seem daunting at first, but Istanbul's public transportation system is extensive and efficient. The Istanbulkart is a smart card that can be used on buses, trams, and ferries, providing a convenient way to get around. Taxis are also widely available, but it is advisable to use reputable companies and ensure the meter is running to avoid excessive charges.

No visit to Istanbul is complete without indulging in its culinary delights. Be sure to try traditional dishes like kebabs, meze, baklava, and the famed Turkish breakfast. Street food is also immensely popular and safe to enjoy, with delicacies like simit, a sesame-covered bread, and roasted chestnuts available at various stalls.

For history enthusiasts, Istanbul is a treasure trove. Must-visit landmarks include the Hagia Sophia, Topkapi Palace, and Basilica Cistern which provide glimpses into the city's Byzantine and Ottoman past. Additionally, taking a Bosphorus cruise offers stunning views of the cityscape and an opportunity to see where continents meet.

Shopping in Istanbul is an experience in and of itself. The Grand Bazaar, one of the largest and oldest covered markets in the world, hosts a myriad of shops selling everything from spices to textiles. Be prepared to haggle respectfully, as it is a common practice. For a more modern shopping experience, Istiklal Avenue offers a mix of international brands and local boutiques.

Lastly, while Turkish people are known for their hospitality and friendliness, learning a few basic Turkish phrases can be immensely helpful and appreciated by the locals. Simple greetings or thank yous can go a long way in enhancing your interactions and overall experience.

By keeping these tips in mind, you'll be well-prepared to navigate and enjoy all that Istanbul, Turkey, has to offer. Whether you are captivated by its rich history, delicious food, or bustling markets, Istanbul is sure to leave an indelible impression on your memory.

Chapter 11: Istanbul Essentials

Local Currency in Istanbul, Turkey

Istanbul, Turkey, is a city where the past seamlessly intertwines with the present, creating a unique blend of cultures and histories. As one navigates through the bustling bazaars, majestic mosques, and vibrant streets, understanding the local currency—the Turkish lira—is essential for a smooth and enriching experience.

The Turkish lira, denoted as TRY, is the official currency of Turkey and is used throughout Istanbul. It comes in various denominations, including banknotes and coins. The banknotes are available in values of 5, 10, 20, 50, 100, and 200 lira, while the coins, known as kurus, come in 1, 5, 10, 25, and 50 kurus, as well as the 1 lira coin. The banknotes feature prominent Turkish figures and landmarks, reflecting the nation's rich heritage and pride.

When exploring Istanbul, it is common to use the lira for everyday transactions, whether you are purchasing a savory simit from a street vendor, enjoying a traditional Turkish tea at a local café, or haggling for goods at the Grand Bazaar. While credit cards are widely accepted in many establishments, especially in more modern or tourist-oriented areas, having cash on hand is advisable for smaller vendors and historic districts where cash payments are more customary.

Currency exchange services are abundant across Istanbul. Visitors can exchange their foreign currencies at banks, specialized exchange offices, hotels, and even certain shops. It is important to compare rates and be aware of potential commission fees that may vary from place to place. ATMs are also conveniently accessible throughout the city and often provide competitive exchange rates. However, it is wise to notify your bank ahead of your travels to avoid any disruptions in service.

Moreover, familiarizing oneself with the current exchange rate is beneficial to ensure fair transactions. As markets can fluctuate, checking the latest rates before converting large amounts can help in making informed decisions.

In summary, the Turkish lira is an integral part of the Istanbul experience, facilitating the myriad of activities and interactions that make this city so captivating. By understanding and using the local currency, visitors can engage more deeply with the cultural and economic tapestry of Istanbul, enhancing their appreciation of this iconic metropolis.Budgeting Tips for Travelers in Istanbul, Turkey

Traveling to Istanbul, Turkey, can be a thrilling experience filled with rich history, vibrant culture, and mouth-watering cuisine. However, like any major city, managing your budget is key to making the most of your trip without breaking the bank. Here are some practical budgeting tips to keep your expenses in check while exploring this magnificent city.

First and foremost, consider visiting during the shoulder seasons, which are April to May and September to October. During these times, the weather is still pleasant, but the tourist crowds and prices are significantly lower compared to the peak summer months. This can help you save on accommodation and reduce the general hustle and bustle.

When it comes to lodging, consider staying in budget-friendly neighborhoods such as Kadikoy or Beyoglu. These areas offer a variety of affordable options like hostels, guesthouses, and boutique hotels. Booking in advance can also secure better rates. Additionally, consider looking for accommodations that include breakfast to reduce one of your daily meal costs.

Public transportation in Istanbul is efficient and economical. The Istanbulkart is a rechargeable card that can be used on buses, trams, ferries, and the metro. It provides a significant discount over purchasing single-ride tickets and is an excellent investment if you plan to explore various parts of the city. Walking is another budget-friendly option, particularly in areas like Sultanahmet and along the Bosphorus, where many attractions are concentrated.

Food is an integral part of the Istanbul experience, and you do not have to splurge to enjoy it. Street food options like simit, a sesame-covered bread, and balik ekmek, a fish sandwich, are delicious and inexpensive. Local markets, such as the Kadikoy Market, offer fresh produce and prepared foods at reasonable prices. Moreover, many local eateries known as lokantas serve traditional Turkish homestyle meals at affordable prices.

For sightseeing, take advantage of the numerous free or low-cost attractions. Historic sites such as the Blue Mosque and the Hippodrome have no entry fees. Even the iconic Hagia Sophia, which now operates as a mosque, can be visited without an admission charge. For other famous attractions that require a ticket, such as Topkapi Palace or the Basilica Cistern, consider purchasing a Museum Pass Istanbul. This pass grants you access to several top sites and can save you money if you plan to visit multiple locations.

In summary, with a few strategic choices, it is possible to fully enjoy the splendors of Istanbul, Turkey, on a budget. Being mindful of when you travel, where you stay, how you get around, what you eat, and which attractions you visit will all contribute to a memorable and cost-effective trip. With these tips, you will be well on your way to experiencing the magic of Istanbul without the financial stress.Istanbul, Turkey, a city that bridges two continents and boasts a rich tapestry of history and culture, is a top destination for travelers from around the world. Despite its many wonders, it is important for visitors to be aware of common scams in order to fully enjoy their experience in this magnificent city.

One frequent scam involves overly friendly strangers who strike up a conversation with tourists. These individuals often pretend to be fellow travelers or locals wanting to practice their English. Once trust is established, they may invite the tourist to a bar or a cafe. Unbeknownst to the visitor, these establishments are complicit in the scam and charge exorbitant prices for drinks or food. When the bill arrives, it can be shockingly high, and refusal to pay often results in intimidating behavior from the staff. To avoid this situation, it is best to be cautious with overly friendly strangers and stick to well-reviewed and reputable establishments.

Another common scam in Istanbul involves taxi drivers. Some drivers may take advantage of unsuspecting tourists by taking longer, out-of-the-way routes or using rigged meters that charge significantly higher fares. To protect oneself from this scam, it is advisable to have a good understanding of the route beforehand, use apps like Google Maps to monitor the journey, and insist on using a metered taxi or a reputable ride-hailing service. Additionally, agreeing on an approximate fare before starting the trip can also mitigate potential overcharging issues.

Fake goods and counterfeit money are additional concerns. Street vendors and some markets may sell imitation brand-name goods at prices that seem too good to be true. While this might seem like a bargain, the quality is often poor and the purchase may not be worth the money spent. Similarly, receiving counterfeit money as change is a risk. Tourists should familiarize themselves with Turkish currency and verify the authenticity of notes received. When possible, it is beneficial to use a credit card at reputable establishments to avoid handling potentially fake currency altogether.

Moreover, another prevalent scam entails fake carpet shops. Tourists are often approached by friendly locals who invite them to visit their "family carpet shop" for a tea and a special offer. These shops typically employ high-pressure sales tactics to convince visitors to buy overpriced carpets purportedly made by local artisans. The carpets might not be genuine or worth the price demanded. It is crucial to shop for carpets and other crafts at well-known, reliable stores recommended by trusted sources or guides.

Lastly, a subtle but common scam involves the classic shell game or variations of it, played in tourist-heavy areas. Scam artists entice onlookers with what appears to be an easy chance to win money. In reality, these games are rigged, and accomplices in the crowd help the operator facilitate the deception. The best way to avoid falling victim to this scam is simply not to engage and to keep a safe distance from such street games.

By being aware of these common scams and exercising caution, visitors to Istanbul can ensure that their time in this enchanting city is as enjoyable and memorable as possible. Istanbul's vibrant culture, historic sites, and warm hospitality await those who explore it with an informed and vigilant approach.Istanbul, Turkey is a mesmerizing city that bridges Europe and Asia, blending rich history with a vibrant modern culture. However, when traveling to Istanbul, it is essential to be well-prepared to ensure a safe and healthy visit. Here are some useful health and safety tips for travelers.

Before traveling, it is advisable to check for any required vaccinations. While no specific immunizations are mandatory for entry into Turkey, it is wise to be up-to-date on routine vaccinations such as measles, mumps, and rubella (MMR) and tetanus-diphtheria-pertussis (Tdap). Additionally, it is worth considering vaccines for hepatitis A and B, typhoid, and rabies, particularly if you plan to engage in outdoor activities or stay in rural areas.

In Istanbul, it is generally safe to drink bottled water, which is widely available and inexpensive. Although tap water is treated and safe for brushing teeth and washing hands, it is best to avoid drinking it directly to prevent any gastrointestinal discomfort.

When exploring the city, be aware of common traveler's safety tips. Istanbul is a bustling city, so be cautious of your belongings, especially in crowded areas like the Grand Bazaar, Istiklal Street, and Sultanahmet. Pickpocketing can occur, so it is wise to use a money belt or a secure bag and avoid displaying valuable items like expensive jewelry or electronics.

Transportation in Istanbul is well-developed, but traffic can be heavy and chaotic. When using public transportation, such as trams, buses, and ferries, be mindful of your surroundings, and avoid traveling during peak hours if possible. Taxis are also a convenient option, but always ensure the meter is running to avoid being overcharged. It might be helpful to use ride-hailing apps for added security and straightforward transactions.

Healthcare facilities in Istanbul are of high quality, with many doctors and staff speaking English, especially in private hospitals. It is prudent to carry comprehensive travel insurance that covers medical expenses, including any potential emergencies. Pharmacies are plentiful and well-stocked with both prescription and over-the-counter medications. However, it is a good idea to bring a small first-aid kit and any personal medications you might require during your trip.

Weather can vary significantly depending on the season, so dress appropriately to match the climate. Summers can be hot and humid, so light clothing, sunglasses, and sunscreen are essential. In contrast, winters can be cold and damp, necessitating warm clothing and an umbrella.

Respecting local customs and traditions is crucial while in Istanbul. Turkey is a predominantly Muslim country, and visitors should dress modestly, particularly when visiting religious sites like mosques. Women may be required to cover their heads, shoulders, and knees at these locations. Following these guidelines not only shows respect but also enriches your cultural experience in Istanbul.

Overall, Istanbul is a wonderful city to explore, offering a wealth of historical sites, delicious cuisine, and a unique blend of cultures. By following these health and safety tips, travelers can enjoy a memorable and safe experience in this enchanting city.Cultural Do's and Don'ts in Istanbul, Turkey

Istanbul, Turkey, a vibrant city that bridges Europe and Asia, is rich in history, culture, and tradition. When visiting this dynamic metropolis, being mindful of cultural norms can enhance your experience and show respect for the local population. Here are some important cultural do's and don'ts to keep in mind.

Do dress modestly. Istanbul is a city where tradition and modernity coexist, but it leans towards conservative dress, especially in areas like mosques and traditional neighborhoods. Women should cover their shoulders and knees, while men should avoid wearing shorts in such places. Carrying a scarf to cover your head when visiting mosques is also recommended.

Do show respect in places of worship. Mosques are integral to the cultural fabric of Istanbul. When visiting, take off your shoes before entering and keep noise to a minimum. Avoid visiting during prayer times, particularly on Fridays, and be sure to ask for permission before taking photos inside.

Do embrace local customs. Practicing phrases like "Merhaba" for hello, "Lutfen" for please, and "Tesekkur ederim" for thank you can go a long way in building rapport with locals. Showing appreciation for Turkish hospitality, such as accepting tea or coffee when offered, is also courteous and enhances cultural exchange.

Do bargain politely. In markets and bazaars, bargaining is a common practice. Approach it with good humor and respect. Start by offering a lower price than what is asked, and be prepared to meet somewhere in the middle. However, do not insist if the seller is firm on their price.

Don't point the soles of your feet at people or religious objects. This is considered disrespectful. When sitting, try to keep your feet flat on the ground and avoid putting them on furniture.

Don't engage in public displays of affection. While Istanbul is more liberal than some parts of Turkey, it is still advisable to avoid excessive physical affection in public. Holding hands is generally acceptable, but kissing or hugging in public may attract unwanted attention.

Don't talk about sensitive topics. Politics, particularly involving the Turkish government or historical events such as the Armenian Genocide, can be very sensitive subjects. Unless you are well-acquainted with your conversation partner and sure of their comfort level, it is best to steer clear of these topics.

Don't refuse food and drink offerings outright. Turkish culture is known for its hospitality, and refusing an offer of food or drink can be seen as impolite. If you truly cannot accept, it is best to politely decline with a valid reason, such as dietary restrictions.

By following these cultural do's and don'ts, you will find your visit to Istanbul not only enjoyable but also deeply enriching. Respecting local customs and traditions helps to bridge cultural gaps and fosters mutual respect and understanding. Enjoy your journey through this remarkable city, where every street and alley whispers tales of its diverse and storied past.Important Social Norms in Istanbul, Turkey

Istanbul, Turkey, is a city of rich history and diverse cultural influences, making it a unique blend of East meets West. Understanding the social norms in Istanbul is essential for anyone visiting or planning to stay in this vibrant metropolis. These norms shape daily interactions and the overall social atmosphere of the city.

One of the most significant social norms in Istanbul is the emphasis on politeness and respect. In Turkish culture, it is important to greet others warmly and use polite forms of address. When meeting someone, a firm handshake accompanied by maintaining eye contact is customary. In more traditional settings, a slight bow of the head may also be appropriate. Addressing people with titles such as Mr or Mrs followed by their first name or using Bey for men and Hanim for women as a more formal address shows respect and politeness.

Hospitality is a cornerstone of Turkish culture, and this is no different in Istanbul. Visitors to the city often find themselves invited to homes or offered tea in shops and public places. Accepting these invitations and showing gratitude is seen as polite. It is also customary to remove your shoes when entering someone's home and to bring a small gift as a token of appreciation.

Another important social norm revolves around public behavior and modesty. In Istanbul, public displays of affection are generally frowned upon, especially in more conservative areas. While Istanbul is a modern and cosmopolitan city, dressing modestly is still appreciated. For women, this may mean covering shoulders and avoiding revealing clothing, particularly when visiting religious sites such as mosques.

Respect for elders is deeply ingrained in Turkish society. In Istanbul, it is expected that younger people show deference to older individuals by giving up seats in public transportation, opening doors, and addressing them with respectful language. This respect for older generations reflects the broader value placed on family and community in Turkish culture.

Additionally, Istanbulites place great importance on mealtime etiquette. Meals are viewed as a time for family and social bonding. It is customary to start eating only after the host has invited everyone to begin. Complimenting the cook and tasting a bit of everything offered is seen as polite. Tea, traditionally served in small tulip-shaped glasses, is a ubiquitous part of social interactions and is often offered multiple times a day.

In summary, understanding and adhering to these social norms can greatly enhance one's experience in Istanbul, Turkey. Politeness, hospitality, modesty, respect for elders, and proper mealtime etiquette are key aspects of daily life in this city. By embracing these customs, visitors can navigate the social landscape of Istanbul with ease and make meaningful connections with its warm and welcoming residents.Istanbul, Turkey, a city straddling two continents, is a captivating blend of cultures, histories, and languages. For any visitor, learning a few basic Turkish phrases can greatly enhance the experience of exploring this vibrant metropolis. Turkish, the predominant language spoken in Istanbul, is known for its melodic cadence and rich lexicon.

When navigating the city's bustling streets, markets, and historic sites, polite greetings go a long way. A simple "Merhaba" meaning "Hello" can open doors and hearts. For a more formal greeting, "Gunaydin" meaning "Good morning" and "Iyi aksamlar" meaning "Good evening" are useful. Expressing gratitude is equally important; "Tesekkur ederim" meaning "Thank you" shows appreciation, while the more casual "Sagol" can also suffice.

Traveling through the city often involves interactions with locals, especially in places like the Grand Bazaar or during a ferry ride across the Bosporus. Knowing how to ask for help or directions is crucial. "Nasil gidilir?" meaning "How do I get there?" can assist in navigating the labyrinthine streets. Additionally, phrases like "Lutfen" meaning "Please" and "Affedersiniz" meaning "Excuse me" demonstrate respect and politeness.

Dining in Istanbul, with its plethora of culinary delights, becomes even more enjoyable with a few basic phrases. "Menu lutfen" meaning "Menu please" initiates the dining experience, while "Hesap lutfen" meaning "Check please" concludes it. Asking about the food, "Bu yemek nedir?" meaning "What is this dish?" can lead to delightful conversations and discoveries about Turkish cuisine.

Mastering numbers is also practical, especially when shopping or negotiating prices. The first ten numbers, "Bir" through "On," are fundamental. To compliment someone or something, "Cok guzel" meaning "Very beautiful" is often met with a smile and can break cultural barriers.

While English is widely understood in the more touristy parts of Istanbul, making an effort to speak Turkish not only facilitates smoother interactions but also shows cultural appreciation and respect. Each phrase learned and used is a step towards deeper connection with the city and its people. Hence, whether wandering through the ancient streets of Sultanahmet, cruising on the Bosporus, or immersing oneself in the vibrant nightlife of Taksim, these basic phrases create a more enriching and immersive experience in Istanbul, Turkey.Istanbul, Turkey is a city that offers an intriguing blend of rich history and vibrant modernity, bridging two continents. When exploring Istanbul, there are several travel-specific vocabulary terms that enhance the depth of your visit.

One of the most significant terms is "Sultanahmet," the name of the historic neighborhood that houses the Hagia Sophia, the Blue Mosque, and Topkapi Palace. These landmarks are collectively referred to as "cultural keystones," pivotal to understanding Istanbul's past.

A visit to Istanbul would be incomplete without experiencing a "Bosphorus cruise." This term refers to a boat journey along the Bosphorus Strait, offering panoramic views of both the European and Asian sides of the city. This waterway is a vital part of Istanbul's identity, acting as a natural dividing line and a busy shipping route.

The "Grand Bazaar," one of the largest and oldest covered markets in the world, is another essential term. Here, the atmosphere is thick with the scent of spices, the gleam of Turkish lamps, and the hum of traders engaging in the age-old practice of haggling.

"Aya Sofya," the Turkish name for Hagia Sophia, is a place where the layers of Byzantine and Ottoman history converge. Originally a cathedral, later an imperial mosque, and now a museum, it's a term that encapsulates the complexity of Istanbul's religious and cultural transformations.

Another term to know is "Dolmabahce Palace," the epitome of Ottoman grandeur and modernity. This site exemplifies the shift from traditional architecture to European-inspired designs, representing the late Ottoman period where East truly met West.

Istanbul's dynamic nature is also reflected in terms like "Istiklal Street," a bustling pedestrian avenue in the Beyoglu district. This street is symbolic of modern Istanbul, lined with shops, cafes, and historical arcades, making it a microcosm of the city's diversity.

Finally, no lexicon of Istanbul would be complete without "Turkish Bath" or "Hamam." These baths are integral to the local culture, offering visitors a quintessential experience of relaxation and tradition.

Collectively, these travel-specific vocabulary terms enrich the narrative of Istanbul, guiding visitors through a city where ancient traditions and contemporary life effortlessly intertwine.

Chapter 12: Navigating Istanbul's Transport Network

Overview of Public Transport in Istanbul, Turkey

Istanbul, Turkey's largest city, is renowned for its rich history and vibrant culture. It is a bustling metropolis that spans two continents, Europe and Asia, divided by the Bosphorus Strait. With a population exceeding 15 million, efficient public transport is essential to keep the city moving. Fortunately, Istanbul boasts a comprehensive and multi-modal public transport network, which makes navigating this sprawling urban landscape both convenient and accessible.

The backbone of Istanbul's public transport is its extensive network of buses, which are operated by the Istanbul Electric Tram and Tunnel Company, also known as IETT. These buses crisscross the city, providing crucial links between neighborhoods and key transit hubs. Complementing the bus system is the metro, which has expanded significantly in recent years. The metro system currently features multiple lines that connect various parts of the city, offering a fast and reliable alternative to road-based transport, particularly during the notoriously congested rush hours.

Trams are another important component of Istanbul's public transport. The city operates several tramlines, including the historic tram on Istiklal Street, which adds a nostalgic charm while serving practical needs. Modern tramlines, such as the T1 line running from Kabatas to Bagcilar, provide additional connectivity and coverage for residents and tourists alike.

The Marmaray, a rail service that runs underneath the Bosphorus, represents a monumental feat of engineering. This underwater rail line connects the European and Asian sides, significantly reducing travel time across the strait and proving to be a critical commuter route. Similarly, the Metrobus, a bus rapid transit system, operates on dedicated lanes, ensuring punctually and speed even amid heavy traffic conditions.

Ferries also play an essential role, given Istanbul's unique geographical layout. The city's numerous ferry lines traverse the Bosphorus and the Golden Horn, offering scenic and practical routes that link various waterfront districts. This mode of transport not only serves daily commuters but also provides a pleasant and picturesque way for visitors to experience the charm of the city from the water.

In addition to these major modes, Istanbul's public transport network includes funiculars, cable cars, and shared taxis known locally as dolmus. The funiculars connect steep areas, such as from Karakoy to Istiklal Street, while cable cars offer quick rides over shorter distances, often providing stunning views of the cityscape. Dolmus, on the other hand, are usually minibuses or large taxis that follow specific routes and are a popular choice for quick, inexpensive travel.

An essential part of navigating Istanbul's public transport is the Istanbulkart, a contactless smart card that can be used across all forms of public transport. This system simplifies fare payments and is a convenient tool for residents and tourists alike.

Overall, Istanbul's public transport network is a testament to the city's dynamic blend of history and modernity. With a wide array of options spanning land, sea, and underground travel, it ensures that moving through this vibrant and diverse city remains as efficient and enjoyable as possible. The continuous development and expansion of the system underscore Istanbul's commitment to providing a sustainable and efficient transportation solution for its ever-growing population.Istanbul, Turkey, is a city that serves as a rich tapestry of cultures, histories, and traditions. Straddling two continents, Europe and Asia, it uniquely marries the modern and the ancient in a way few other cities can. Utilizing Istanbul effectively involves understanding its diverse and multifaceted nature, which offers something for every traveler.

Firstly, transportation within Istanbul can be navigated through a variety of options, from its extensive tram and metro systems to its iconic ferry rides across the Bosphorus Strait. The Istanbulkart, a reloadable transportation card, can be used on buses, trams, and ferries, making it an essential tool for anyone looking to explore the city efficiently. Taxis and ride-sharing services are also prevalent, but one must always be cautious of potential fare inflation and opt for metered rides.

Accommodations in Istanbul range from luxurious five-star hotels overlooking the Bosphorus to charming boutique hotels in historic neighborhoods like Sultanahmet. For those seeking a more authentic experience, the Airbnb platform offers numerous options, from modern apartments to traditional Ottoman homes.

When it comes to dining, Istanbul is a paradise for food lovers. The local cuisine is a delightful blend of Middle Eastern, Mediterranean, and Central Asian influences. Street food is an integral part of the city's culinary landscape, with must-try items like simit, a sesame-encrusted bread, and doner kebabs readily available. For a more formal dining experience, one can visit the city's numerous restaurants that offer everything from traditional Turkish dishes to international fare. Be sure to visit a meyhane, a traditional Turkish tavern, to enjoy meze and raki, a local anise-flavored spirit.

Shopping is another way to immerse oneself in the vibrant culture of Istanbul. The Grand Bazaar, one of the oldest and largest covered markets in the world, offers an endless array of goods, from textiles and ceramics to jewelry and spices. For a more contemporary shopping experience, Akmerkez or Istinye Park are modern malls featuring international brands.

Cultural and historical attractions are abundant in Istanbul. The Hagia Sophia, a UNESCO World Heritage site, stands as a symbol of the city's storied past, having served as a church, mosque, and now a museum. The Blue Mosque, Topkapi Palace, and the Basilica Cistern are just a few other landmarks that provide insight into the city's rich history. Art enthusiasts can visit museums like the Istanbul Modern or Pera Museum, which offer a contemporary view of Turkish art and culture.

Utilizing Istanbul also means being mindful of its customs and social etiquette. While the city is relatively liberal, it is important to remember that Turkey is a predominantly Muslim country. Modesty in dress, especially when visiting religious sites, and an awareness of the call to prayer times can go a long way in showing respect for local traditions.

In conclusion, using Istanbul to its fullest involves embracing its complexities and contrasts. From efficient transportation and varied accommodations to diverse dining options and rich cultural experiences, the city offers a plethora of opportunities for both leisure and discovery. By understanding and respecting its unique identity, visitors can truly appreciate what makes Istanbul a global treasure.Istanbul, Turkey is a city that beautifully blends the old with the new, where ancient traditions coexist with modern advancements. This unique fusion is also reflected in the abundance of reliable services available to its residents and visitors alike. From healthcare to transportation, and from hospitality to technology, Istanbul offers a robust and dependable infrastructure that enhances the quality of life and ensures a comfortable stay for anyone who visits.

Healthcare services in Istanbul are renowned for their high standards and accessibility. The city is home to a number of internationally accredited hospitals and clinics, staffed by skilled medical professionals who provide top-notch care. The public healthcare system is supported by private establishments that cater to a variety of needs, offering everything from routine check-ups to advanced medical treatments with state-of-the-art facilities.

Transportation within Istanbul is another area where reliability shines through. The city boasts an extensive and efficient public transportation network, including buses, trams, and the metro, which makes navigating the sprawling metropolis relatively simple. Recent investments in infrastructure have also led to the development of new metro lines and expressways, further easing congestion and making travel more efficient. For those preferring private transportation, ride-sharing services and taxis are readily available and can be conveniently accessed via mobile applications.

Moreover, Istanbul is a city that takes pride in its hospitality industry. The city's hotels, restaurants, and tourist services are known for their high standards of customer care and professionalism. Whether staying in a luxury hotel overlooking the Bosphorus or enjoying a meal at a family-run restaurant in a bustling neighborhood, visitors can expect consistent quality and service. Tour operators and guides in the city are well-versed in multiple languages and have a deep understanding of the city's history and culture, which ensures a rich and informative experience for all tourists.

In the realm of technology, Istanbul has not lagged behind either. A growing hub for startups and technological innovation, the city provides reliable internet and communication services. Numerous co-working spaces and business centers equipped with modern amenities cater to entrepreneurs and professionals who seek a conducive environment to work and innovate.

Overall, Istanbul, Turkey, despite its vast size and vibrant chaos, manages to offer a network of reliable services that cover all facets of daily life. This reliability is one of many factors that make the city an attractive destination for both living and visiting, offering modern comforts amidst a backdrop of historic wonders.Tips for Using Taxis in Istanbul, Turkey

Navigating Istanbul, one of the most vibrant and historic cities in the world, can be an adventure in itself. With its bustling streets and winding alleys, sometimes the most efficient way to get around is by taxi. Here are some essential tips for using taxis in Istanbul to ensure a smooth and pleasant experience.

Firstly, it is crucial to understand the basic taxi fare system in Istanbul. Taxis in this city operate using a meter, which starts at a base fare and increases with distance and time. Make sure the driver starts the meter at the beginning of your journey; the initial fare should be clearly visible. Avoid entering taxis that do not display a meter, as this can lead to overcharging. It is also advisable to carry small denominations of the local currency, the Turkish Lira, as not all drivers will have change for larger bills.

One of the most effective ways to avoid misunderstandings or communication issues is to have your destination written down, especially if you do not speak Turkish. Many taxi drivers may not speak English fluently, so showing the address can help ensure you reach the correct location. Additionally, naming a prominent landmark near your destination can be helpful, as drivers are often more familiar with well-known sites.

While hailing a taxi on the street is common, using a taxi app can offer added security and convenience. Apps like Bitaksi and iTaksi allow you to request a ride from your smartphone and provide features such as tracking your route and making cashless payments. These apps can also provide you with the estimated fare before you confirm the ride, helping you avoid any surprises.

During peak hours and in busy areas, traffic congestion can significantly increase travel time and cost. Plan your trips to avoid rush hours if possible, typically from 7:00 to 10:00 in the morning and 5:00 to 8:00 in the evening. This consideration can save you both money and frustration. Additionally, be aware that some routes may require crossing one of the city's bridges or tunnels, which often have tolls. These tolls are usually added to your final fare, so it can be helpful to ask about any additional charges before starting your journey.

Tipping is customary but not mandatory in Istanbul. If you are satisfied with the service, rounding up the fare or leaving a small tip, around 10 percent, is appreciated. However, do not feel obligated to tip if the service was unsatisfactory or if you believe you were overcharged.

Lastly, always be vigilant about your belongings. Keep your valuable items in sight and take your phone, wallet, and bag with you when you exit the taxi. This simple precaution can prevent any potential issues, ensuring a safe and enjoyable ride.

By following these tips, using taxis in Istanbul can be a convenient and efficient way to explore the city. Whether you are heading to the bustling Grand Bazaar, the majestic Blue Mosque, or simply navigating the charming streets, being well-prepared will help make your journey smooth and enjoyable.Rental Tips for Istanbul, Turkey

Istanbul, Turkey is a captivating city that bridges Europe and Asia, offering a rich tapestry of history, culture, and modern amenities. If you are considering renting a property in this dynamic metropolis, there are several essential tips to keep in mind to ensure a smooth and satisfying experience.

First and foremost, it is crucial to understand the distinct neighborhoods of Istanbul before making a rental decision. Areas such as Beyoglu, Kadikoy, and Besiktas each have their unique charm and characteristics. Beyoglu, known for its vibrant nightlife and historical landmarks, is ideal for those seeking an energetic environment. Kadikoy, on the Asian side, offers a more laid-back atmosphere with its local markets and seaside promenades. Besiktas is popular among both locals and expats for its central location and lively waterfront. By exploring these neighborhoods, you can find the one that best matches your lifestyle preferences.

Another important tip is to set a realistic budget. Istanbul's rental prices can vary significantly depending on the neighborhood, size, and condition of the property. Setting a clear budget will help narrow down your options and prevent overspending. Additionally, be mindful of the fluctuating exchange rates if you are renting in a foreign currency.

When searching for a rental property, utilizing online platforms and local real estate agencies can be very effective. Websites such as Sahibinden.com and Hurriyet Emlak are popular choices for finding listings. Engaging with a trusted real estate agent can also provide valuable insights and assist with negotiations, especially if you are unfamiliar with the Turkish language or local market practices.

Inspecting the property thoroughly before signing any agreement is essential. Pay attention to the condition of the building, the functionality of appliances, and the availability of amenities like heating and air conditioning. It is also advisable to check the neighborhood during different times of the day to understand the noise levels, traffic, and overall environment.

Understanding the terms of the rental agreement is critical. Ensure that all the terms related to the duration of the lease, payment schedules, maintenance responsibilities, and any additional costs are clearly outlined in the contract. It is wise to have the agreement reviewed by a legal professional to safeguard your interests.

Furthermore, be aware of the deposit requirements. Landlords in Istanbul usually request a security deposit equivalent to one or two months' rent. Make sure that the terms for the return of the deposit are explicitly stated in the agreement to avoid any future disputes.

Finally, building a good relationship with your landlord can go a long way. Clear communication and mutual respect can lead to a more pleasant and cooperative rental experience.

By considering these rental tips, you can navigate the Istanbul rental market with confidence and find a home that meets your needs and enhances your stay in this remarkable city.Driving in Istanbul, Turkey

Driving in Istanbul, Turkey, presents a unique blend of modern city driving challenges combined with the cultural richness that the city exudes. With a population of over 15 million people, Istanbul is one of the most populous cities in the world, and this is evident in its traffic conditions. The city's roads are a mix of ancient, narrow streets and expansive, modern highways, creating a dynamic driving environment that requires both skill and patience.

One of the first things a driver will notice is the sheer volume of vehicles on the road. Istanbul's traffic can be daunting, especially during peak hours when congestion is at its worst. The Bosphorus bridges, which connect the European and Asian sides of the city, are notorious for heavy traffic. Despite modern advancements and infrastructure improvements, rush hour traffic remains a significant challenge. It is not uncommon for a journey that would typically take 15 minutes to extend to an hour or more during these busy periods.

Navigating the streets of Istanbul also demands a certain level of assertiveness. Local drivers are known for their assertive driving style, often weaving through traffic, honking horns, and making swift lane changes. While this can be intimidating for those not used to such driving conditions, it is essential to stay calm and focused. Defensive driving and a heightened awareness of your surroundings will go a long way in ensuring a safe journey.

Furthermore, Istanbul's unique blend of European and Asian influences means that drivers can encounter a diverse range of road users, from modern cars and motorcycles to more traditional forms of transportation like scooters and bicycles. Pedestrian activity is also high, with people frequently crossing streets at unexpected points. This adds another layer of complexity to driving in the city, necessitating constant vigilance.

Parking in Istanbul can be another significant challenge. Finding a parking spot, especially in popular areas such as Taksim Square, Sultanahmet, or near the Grand Bazaar, can be particularly difficult. Many locals rely on private parking lots or valet services to alleviate this issue. Additionally, narrow streets in older parts of the city often mean that parking spots are limited and difficult to navigate.

Despite these challenges, driving in Istanbul also offers unique rewards. The city is a treasure trove of history, and driving through its streets allows one to witness a blend of architectural marvels, from ancient Byzantine churches and Ottoman mosques to modern skyscrapers. The scenic routes along the Bosphorus offer breathtaking views of both natural beauty and historic landmarks like the Hagia Sophia, Topkapi Palace, and Dolmabahce Palace.

Moreover, having a car in Istanbul provides the flexibility to explore beyond the city limits. The surrounding areas of Istanbul, such as the Princes' Islands, Belgrad Forest, and the coastal towns along the Black Sea, are easily accessible by car, offering a refreshing escape from the hustle and bustle of city life.

In conclusion, driving in Istanbul, Turkey, is both a challenging and rewarding experience. While the traffic conditions and assertive driving styles can be intimidating, the opportunity to explore such a vibrant and historically rich city at one's own pace is a privilege. With careful attention, patience, and a bit of local knowledge, driving in Istanbul can be an unforgettable part of your journey in this extraordinary city.

Chapter 13: Istanbul Insider Tips

Local Insights: Istanbul, Turkey

Istanbul, Turkey's bustling metropolis, is a city where the historic past intertwines seamlessly with the contemporary present. Straddling two continents, Europe and Asia, Istanbul boasts a unique geographical position that has played a crucial role in its rich, diverse history. This transcontinental city embodies a vibrant cultural mosaic shaped by myriad civilizations, including the Greeks, Romans, Byzantines, and Ottomans.

The heart of Istanbul beats in its historic districts, such as Sultanahmet, where the iconic Hagia Sophia and the Blue Mosque dominate the skyline. Hagia Sophia, once a church, later a mosque, and now a museum, stands as a testament to the city's layered history and architectural marvel. Nearby, the Blue Mosque's six minarets and cascading domes exemplify classical Ottoman design, drawing visitors and worshippers alike.

To truly experience local life, one must stroll through the bustling Grand Bazaar, one of the world's largest and oldest covered markets. Here, the scent of spices mingles with vibrant displays of ceramics, textiles, and jewelry, offering a sensory feast that encapsulates Istanbul's trading spirit. The nearby Spice Bazaar, with its aromatic herbs and colorful array of edibles, further amplifies the city's colorful commercial heritage.

Istanbul's neighborhoods each tell their own story. Beyoğlu, with its bohemian atmosphere and the pedestrian-friendly Istiklal Avenue, buzzes with art galleries, cafes, and lively nightlife. The district of Kadıköy on the Asian side offers a more relaxed vibe, with trendy cafes, antique shops, and the bustling Fish Market displaying local flavors.

The Bosphorus, the city's lifeline, offers a unique perspective of Istanbul. A ferry ride along this strait not only showcases stunning views of palaces and fortresses but also highlights daily life in waterfront communities. The sound of seagulls, the sight of fishing boats, and the gentle sway of the water add to the city's distinctive rhythm.

Istanbul's culinary scene is an otherworldly journey that reflects its diverse cultural tapestry. From the famous simit vendors on every corner to the sophisticated Ottoman cuisine in fine dining restaurants, the food here offers something for everyone. Do not miss the opportunity to try local favorites like kebabs, mezes, and baklava. Each bite tells a story of tradition and innovation.

Amidst its ancient wonders, Istanbul is also a modern metropolis. Skyscrapers, contemporary art galleries, and chic boutiques indicate a city progressing forward while honoring its past. This blend of old and new creates a dynamic urban fabric that is both complex and inviting.

In essence, Istanbul is a city that transcends time, where every street and building whispers stories of past eras while embracing the future. Its unique position as a bridge between continents makes it a melting pot of cultures, ideas, and histories, captivating visitors and residents alike with its endless charm and depth. To understand Istanbul is to engage with a city that is constantly evolving, yet firmly rooted in the legacy of its rich, multifaceted heritage.Hidden Gems in Istanbul, Turkey

Istanbul, Turkey is a city steeped in history and culture, often celebrated for its impressive landmarks like the Hagia Sophia, the Blue Mosque, and the Grand Bazaar. However, beyond these well-trodden tourist trails lies a wealth of hidden gems waiting to be explored. These lesser-known spots offer a more intimate glimpse into the life and soul of this ancient city.

One such hidden gem is Balat, a historic neighborhood on the European side of Istanbul. Known for its vibrant, colorful houses and steep, cobblestone streets, Balat is a feast for the eyes. The area has a bohemian vibe, with numerous antique shops, quaint cafes, and artisan workshops. Balat's diversity is also reflected in its architecture, where

Orthodox churches, synagogues, and mosques stand side by side, each telling a story of a multicultural past.

Another secret treasure is the Basilica Cistern, an underground marvel located near the more famous Hagia Sophia. This ancient, subterranean structure dates back to the 6th century and was originally designed to store water for the city. As visitors descend into the cool, cavernous space, they are greeted by the sight of hundreds of illuminated columns, casting ghostly reflections in the shallow waters below. The atmosphere is otherworldly, making the Basilica Cistern a must-visit for those seeking a unique experience in Istanbul.

For a peaceful retreat from the bustling city streets, Emirgan Park offers a serene escape. Located along the Bosphorus Strait, this expansive park is particularly famous for its annual Tulip Festival in April, where millions of tulips bloom in a riot of colors. The park also features charming Ottoman-style pavilions, scenic walking paths, and picturesque picnic spots, providing a perfect setting for a leisurely day out.

Foodies looking to explore Istanbul's culinary landscape should not miss the Kadikoy Market on the Asian side of the city. Unlike the more touristy markets, Kadikoy offers an authentic taste of local life. The market is brimming with fresh produce, spices, and traditional Turkish delights. Small, family-owned eateries serve up mouthwatering dishes like manti, a type of Turkish dumpling, and simit, a sesame-covered bread. The lively atmosphere and warm hospitality make it a pleasure to wander through the stalls and discover new flavors.

For those intrigued by Istanbul's artistic side, the Istanbul Modern Art Museum is a hidden jewel. Tucked away in the Karakoy district, this museum showcases contemporary Turkish art alongside international works. It provides a refreshing contrast to the historical sites and offers a window into the modern creative spirit of this ever-evolving city.

In conclusion, while Istanbul's iconic landmarks are certainly worth visiting, there is a treasure trove of hidden gems that offer a deeper and more authentic experience of this captivating city. From historic neighborhoods and underground cisterns to tranquil parks and vibrant markets, Istanbul's lesser-known attractions are a testament to its rich tapestry of history, culture, and modernity. These hidden gems invite travelers to step off the beaten path and discover the unique charm of Istanbul, Turkey.Istanbul, Turkey is a city renowned for its rich history and blend of cultures, but beyond its celebrated sites like the Hagia Sophia and the Blue Mosque, it also offers a plethora of unusual attractions that provide a glimpse into its diverse and vibrant character. These hidden gems, tucked away from the usual tourist trails, reveal an intriguing side of Istanbul that is sure to captivate the curious traveler.

One such attraction is the Basilica Cistern, a subterranean marvel that dates back to the sixth century. This ancient underground water reservoir, built by Byzantine Emperor Justinian I, is a forest of marble columns—336 in total—rising from the still waters. Dimly lit and echoing with the sound of dripping water, the cistern offers an eerie yet magical atmosphere. Among its many columns, two feature Medusa heads serving as bases, their origins and purpose shrouded in mystery.

Another unusual spot is the Museum of Innocence, created by Nobel laureate Orhan Pamuk. This museum is an extension of his novel with the same title, portraying the fictional love story between Kemal and Füsun through a collection of everyday objects from Istanbul of the 1970s and 80s. Each item is meticulously arranged to evoke the poignant narrative of the book, allowing visitors to immerse themselves in the intimate world of its characters. The museum is a testament to the power of storytelling and the nostalgia of a bygone era.

For those intrigued by the macabre, the Crimean Memorial Church offers an unexpected slice of Gothic architecture in the heart of Istanbul. Built to honor British soldiers who fought in the Crimean

War, this Anglican church stands out with its dark stone exterior and stained-glass windows. It seems almost out of place amid the city's predominantly Ottoman and Byzantine architecture, providing a stark contrast that prompts reflection on the complexities of history.

Nature and tranquility await at Yıldız Park, one of Istanbul's largest urban parks. Away from the bustling streets, this green oasis offers winding paths, serene ponds, and an abundance of flora. The park encompasses the historic Yıldız Pavilion and Malta Köşkü, both of which are stunning examples of Ottoman architecture. It is the perfect spot for a leisurely stroll, a picnic, or just a moment of respite from the city's constant motion.

Lastly, the quirky Istanbul Toy Museum beckons to both young and old. Housed in a charming historical mansion, the museum boasts an extensive collection of toys from different eras and countries, meticulously curated by poet and author Sunay Akın. Each room is designed to evoke a sense of wonder, filled with dolls, model trains, and other childhood treasures. The museum not only celebrates the joy of play but also serves as a cultural chronicle, highlighting the evolution of toys over the years.

In summary, Istanbul, Turkey is a city of contrasts and surprises, where ancient history intersects with the avant-garde. Beyond its iconic landmarks, these unusual attractions offer unique insights and experiences for those willing to explore the city's lesser-known corners. Whether it is delving into an underground cistern, wandering through a poignant storytelling museum, or enjoying a picturesque park, there is no shortage of fascinating sites waiting to be discovered in Istanbul.Secret Spots where the City Name is Istanbul, Turkey

Istanbul, Turkey, is a city that seamlessly merges the old with the new, the East with the West, and history with modernity. While it boasts well-known landmarks like the Hagia Sophia, the Blue Mosque, and the Grand Bazaar, the city hides a multitude of secret spots that capture the essence of its rich and diverse culture. For the intrepid traveler, these hidden gems offer a more intimate glimpse into Istanbul's soul away from the bustling crowds.

One such secret spot is the Arnavutkoy neighborhood. Nestled along the Bosphorus, this charming area is often overshadowed by its more famous neighbors. Arnavutkoy features narrow streets lined with traditional Ottoman houses, and it is a perfect place to take a leisurely stroll. The cafés and seafood restaurants here provide a delightful respite and a chance to savor local flavors in a quieter setting.

Cihangir, a district favored by artists and writers, is another hidden treasure. Steeped in a bohemian atmosphere, it has narrow streets filled with quirky boutiques, antique shops, and cozy cafés. Visitors can relax in one of its eclectic coffee spots or take in the magnificent views of the Bosphorus from the small but enchanting Cihangir Park.

For a taste of the mystical, the Rustem Pasha Mosque offers a tranquil escape. Unlike its more famous counterparts, this mosque is often overlooked by tourists. However, it is a masterpiece of Ottoman architecture, adorned with exquisite Iznik tiles that cover its interior. A visit here provides a serene environment for reflection and an appreciation of the intricate artistry that defines much of Istanbul's historical architecture.

The Balat and Fener neighborhoods offer a journey back in time. These areas are known for their colorful houses, winding streets, and historic buildings. Once home to Greek Orthodox and Jewish communities, they are filled with old-world charm. Wandering through these neighborhoods feels like stepping into a different era, with every corner revealing unique stories of Istanbul's multicultural past.

Lastly, the Princes' Islands, just a short ferry ride from the mainland, provide a peaceful retreat from the city's hustle and bustle. Büyükada, the largest of the islands, is car-free, promoting exploration by bike or horse-drawn carriage. The serene landscapes, historic mansions, and clear blue waters offer a perfect day trip back in time to a place where life moves at a slower pace.

Istanbul's secret spots serve as a reminder of its expansive history and vibrant culture. These hidden gems, away from the crowds, offer an authentic experience, allowing visitors to connect deeply with the city's multifaceted identity. Whether it's through exploring charming neighborhoods, discovering architectural masterpieces, or enjoying tranquil escapes, these lesser-known locales reveal the true essence of Istanbul in ways that celebrated landmarks might not.

Chapter 14: Final Reflections on Istanbul

Istanbul, Turkey, is a city brimming with history, culture, and beauty, offering a captivating blend of the ancient and the modern. Straddling two continents, Europe and Asia, Istanbul's unique geographical position makes it a crossroads of civilizations. Visitors can experience this rich cultural tapestry through the city's myriad attractions.

The Hagia Sophia stands as a testament to the city's architectural grandeur. Originally built as a Byzantine cathedral, later converted into a mosque, and now serving as a museum, it encapsulates Istanbul's complex history. Just a short walk away, the Blue Mosque dazzles with its stunning blue tiles and impressive domes, while the Topkapi Palace offers a glimpse into the opulent lives of the Ottoman sultans.

The bustling Grand Bazaar is a sensory overload, with its labyrinthine lanes filled with vendors selling everything from spices to textiles. Equally vibrant is the Spice Bazaar, where the aroma of exotic spices and herbs fills the air. For those seeking a more tranquil experience, a ferry ride along the Bosphorus provides breathtaking views of the city's skyline, adorned with minarets and ancient castles.

Modern Istanbul is no less intriguing. Taksim Square and Istiklal Avenue are the heart of contemporary life, featuring a lively mix of shops, restaurants, and cultural venues. The city's culinary scene is diverse and delectable, offering everything from traditional Turkish dishes like kebabs and baklava to international cuisine.

The city's public transportation system, including trams, metro, and ferries, makes exploring its diverse neighborhoods convenient and enjoyable. Each district, from the historic Sultanahmet to the chic Nisantasi, has its own unique charm and attractions.

In summary, Istanbul, Turkey, is a city where east meets west, history mingles with modernity, and every corner has a story to tell. Whether one is wandering through ancient palaces, haggling in bustling bazaars, or enjoying a leisurely Bosphorus cruise, Istanbul promises an unforgettable experience.Encouragement to Explore Istanbul, Turkey

Istanbul, Turkey, is a city like no other. Straddling two continents and showcasing a blend of cultures, it offers a unique experience to every traveler. If you are mulling over your next travel destination, let Istanbul be your choice, for it holds an intoxicating allure that calls out to the explorer in all of us.

Begin your journey in the historic heart of the city, Sultanahmet, where ancient wonders await. The Hagia Sophia, once a church, later a mosque, and now a museum, stands as a testament to the city's rich and varied history. Its massive dome, adorned with mosaics, leaves visitors awestruck. Nearby, the Blue Mosque, with its six minarets and intricate blue-tiled interior, continues to function as a place of worship, inviting both the curious and the devout.

For a taste of opulence, visit the Topkapi Palace, the former residence of Ottoman sultans. Walking through its lavish courtyards and halls, one can almost hear the whispers of history. The palace also houses the Topkapi dagger and the 86-carat Spoonmaker's Diamond, offering a glimpse into the splendor of a bygone era.

The Grand Bazaar is a must-visit for those who crave the thrill of discovery. One of the largest and oldest covered markets in the world, it consists of thousands of shops selling everything from carpets and jewelry to spices and antiques. Navigating its labyrinthine alleys, you will inevitably be enticed by the aroma of exotic spices and the vibrant colors of handcrafted items.

Do not miss out on the Bosphorus Strait, which divides the city into its European and Asian sides. A ferry ride across this enchanting waterway reveals stunning views of the cityscape, with Ottoman mansions on one shore and modern skyscrapers on the other. Each bend in the river offers new perspectives and an appreciation for Istanbul's role as a bridge between worlds.

Istanbul's culinary scene is another dimension of its charm, blending flavors from various regions of Turkey and beyond. Savoring a doner kebab, indulging in a Turkish delight, or sipping tea by the Bosphorus are simple yet delightful experiences that stay with you long after the journey ends.

Overall, Istanbul is a city that invites you to explore, to wander through its streets, and to lose yourself in its stories. The combination of its historical significance, cultural richness, and modern vibrancy creates a mosaic that is endlessly fascinating. In choosing Istanbul as your destination, you are embarking on an adventure that promises to be as rewarding as it is memorable. So pack your bags, follow the call of this mesmerizing city, and allow Istanbul, Turkey, to reveal its wonders to you.Further Reading: Istanbul, Turkey

Istanbul, Turkey, is a city steeped in history, culture, and a unique blend of traditions that span both Europe and Asia. As one of the most iconic cities in the world, Istanbul offers a myriad of opportunities for further reading to anyone interested in its rich past and vibrant present.

For those wishing to delve into the historical significance of Istanbul, there are numerous texts that explore the city from its ancient roots as Byzantium through its transformation into Constantinople, and finally into the Istanbul of today. Works such as "Istanbul: Memories and the City" by Orhan Pamuk provide a deeply personal and literary exploration of the citys evolution through the eyes of one of its most beloved writers. Pamuks narrative captures the essence of Istanbuls neighborhoods, evoking the soul of the city as only a native can.

Additionally, historians may appreciate text like "Lost to the West" by Lars Brownworth, which recounts the rise and fall of the Byzantine Empire, with a particular focus on Constantinoples pivotal role. This work elucidates the power struggles, architectural grandeur, and cultural shifts that have left an indelible mark on Istanbul.

For a more architectural perspective, "Strolling Through Istanbul: The Classic Guide to the City" by Hilary Sumner-Boyd and John Freely is an essential read. This guide offers detailed insights into the citys iconic structures, from the Hagia Sophia and Topkapi Palace to the hidden gems that dot the citys landscape. The book serves not only as a guide but as a comprehensive historical document that captures the architectural splendor of Istanbul.

To understand the contemporary life and ongoing changes in Istanbul, one might turn to works like "Istanbul: City of Majesty at the Crossroads of the World" by Bettany Hughes. This book provides a sweeping narrative that covers everything from the cities founding legends to its current status as a bustling metropolis. Hughes meticulously details Istanbuls legacy and its ongoing transformation in the face of modern challenges.

Lastly, for those interested in the social and political dynamics of modern-day Istanbul, "The Fall of the Turkish Model" by Cihan Tugal offers a critical analysis of recent decades. Tugals examination of political Islam and its intersection with everyday life in Istanbul provides a thought-provoking look at the citys current and future trajectory.

Further reading on Istanbul, Turkey, thus provides a wealth of knowledge that crosses the boundaries of time and disciplines. Whether through historical examination, architectural appreciation, or contemporary analysis, the literature offers a multifaceted view of a city that has stood at the crossroads of civilizations for millennia.Located at the crossroads of Europe and Asia, Istanbul, Turkey, is a vibrant city steeped in history and culture. With its unique blend of modernity and tradition, the city offers a myriad of experiences for both residents and visitors. To navigate through its rich tapestry, various useful websites can enhance your stay and help you make the most of what Istanbul has to offer.

For starters, the official tourism website, GoTurkey, provides comprehensive information about the city's major attractions, events, and travel tips. Whether you are interested in visiting the iconic Hagia Sophia, exploring the bustling Grand Bazaar, or sailing on the Bosphorus, this website offers valuable insights and practical advice.

Another invaluable resource is the website of Istanbul Metropolitan Municipality, which features up-to-date information on public transport, city services, and local regulations. With maps, schedules, and real-time data, it helps both tourists and locals navigate the city efficiently. The site also includes details on municipal initiatives and events, offering a glimpse into the community's vibrant life.

For those interested in the city's cultural scene, the Istanbul Foundation for Culture and Arts (IKSV) website is a treasure trove. It highlights various festivals, concerts, and exhibitions, showcasing Istanbul's dynamic art and cultural landscape. From film festivals to musical performances, the IKSV is dedicated to enriching the city's cultural offerings.

To explore Istanbul's culinary delights, Zomato and Yelp are excellent platforms for discovering top restaurants, cafes, and street food vendors. With user reviews, ratings, and photos, these websites guide you through the city's gastronomic hotspots, ensuring a memorable dining experience.

For accommodations, Booking.com and Airbnb offer a wide range of options, from luxurious hotels to cozy apartments. These platforms allow you to read guest reviews, compare prices, and find the perfect place to stay, tailored to your preferences and budget.

Additionally, the Expat Guide Turkey website is particularly useful for expatriates and long-term visitors. It provides essential information on residency permits, housing, healthcare, and education, assisting newcomers in adjusting to life in Istanbul.

Lastly, the Istanbul Weather website offers accurate weather forecasts, helping you plan your activities and dress appropriately for the city's often unpredictable weather.

In conclusion, Istanbul's rich history, cultural diversity, and culinary treasures make it a fascinating destination. Utilizing these websites will enhance your experience, providing you with the necessary tools to explore and enjoy this magnificent city to the fullest.

Also by Jake Jefferson

Jake's Travel Guides
Jake's Travel Guides: Madrid, Spain
Jake's Travel Guides: Istanbul, Turkey